MARIO VARGAS LLOSA

LITERATURE AND LIFE: WORLD WRITERS

Selected list of titles in this series:

Complete list of titles in the series available from the
publisher on request.

MARIO VARGAS LLOSA

Raymond Leslie Williams

UNGAR • NEW YORK

PQ
8498.32
.A65
Z94
1986

1986
The Ungar Publishing Company
370 Lexington Avenue, New York, NY 10017

Printed in the United States of America

Library of Congress Cataloging-in-Publication Data

Williams, Raymond L.
    Mario Vargas Llosa.

    (Literature and life. World writers)
    Bibliography: p.
    Includes index.
    1. Vargas Llosa, Mario, 1936–   – Criticism and
interpretation.   I. Title.   II. Series.
PQ8498.32.A65Z94   1986   863   86-25016
ISBN 0-8044-2978-2

Slightly altered portions of this work have appeared in *Texas Studies in Literature and Language*, Vol. xix, No. 4, Winter 1977, and reprinted in *Mario Vargas Llosa: A Collection of Critical Essays*, Charles Rossman and Alan Warren Friedman, editors (University of Texas Press, 1978). Copyright © 1977 by the University of Texas Press. Used by permission of the publisher; *Texto crítico* (Vol. V, No. 13, April–June 1979), reprinted in José Miguel Oviedo, *Mario Vargas Llosa* (Madrid: Taurus Ediciones, 1981); and *Chasqui* (Vol. V, No. 2, February 1976).

In memory of Leslie Leo Williams, 1921–75

Contents

Preface

The present study has three principal objectives: to afford the reader a general introduction to and complete overview of Vargas Llosa's writing, to clarify the technical difficulties that his fiction presents to the nonspecialist, and to provide close analysis of his fiction. Although I have devoted some attention to Vargas Llosa's nonfiction, these writings, along with both his essays and his theater, are discussed primarily in relation to his work as a novelist.

Since this study is directed primarily to an English-speaking readership, quotations from Vargas Llosa's texts usually appear from the published English translation (my own translations appear for the few texts not yet published in English). In several instances, however, a closer reading is provided by also including the quotation in the original Spanish. Some passages from *The Cubs*, *Conversation in The Cathedral*, and *The War of the End of the World* appear in both English and Spanish.

In principle, I have avoided specialized terminology. Nevertheless, readers will note some references to recent developments in narratology — namely the work of Gérard Genette, Mikhail Bakhtin, and Mieke Bal — whenever the concepts of these critics might enrich the analysis of a given text. I do occasionally use the term "heteroglossia," which is perhaps best understood by thinking of the Greek roots: "heter," meaning "other," and "glossa," meaning "language." Bakhtin has used this term, referring to the "other languages" or variety of languages that literary texts often assimilate. I also rely occasionally on some useful concepts developed recently by Walter Ong in order to elucidate various aspects of Vargas Llosa's technique. These ideas are explained in the course of this study.

RLW

Acknowledgments

I would like to express my gratitude to my friends and colleagues whose conversations, suggestions, and assistance have been invaluable: John and Carolyn Brushwood, René de Costa, Wayne Fields, Dick Gerdes, John L. Grigsby, James F. Jones, Jr., Roy Kerr, William Kirby, Naomi Lebowitz, Evander Lomke, Wolfgang A. Luchting, Michael Moody, José Miguel Oviedo, Raymond and Martha Souza, Frances Stadler, Cristie Tober, Brian Vandenberg, Richard Walter, and Pamela Williams. I appreciate the research leave granted to me by the Faculty of Arts and Sciences of Washington University in order to complete this project, and the Graduate School for the funds which supported it.

Acknowledgments

Chronology

1936   Born in Arequipa, Peru.
1937   Moves to Cochabamba, Bolivia, where he is reared by his mother and grandparents.
1945   Returns to Peru (town of Piura).
1946   Moves to Lima.
1950–52 In Leoncio Prado Military School, Lima. In 1952 returns to Piura, where he works part-time for newspapers and writes the play *La huida del Inca* (The Flight of the Inca).
1953   Enters San Marcos University to study law.
1956   Publication of first stories in newspapers.
1958   Awarded prize for short story from *Revue Française* and travels to Paris. Makes first trip to Amazon jungles of Peru. After return from Paris to Lima, goes to Spain to study literature at the Universidad Central de Madrid.
1959   Publishes *Los jefes* (The Leaders). Awarded Leopoldo Alas Prize. Moves from Spain to Paris with his wife, Julia Urquidi.
1962   Awarded Biblioteca Breve Prize. Begins writing articles in newspapers and magazines with regularity.
1963   Publishes *La ciudad y los perros (The Time of the Hero)*. Awarded Premio de la Crítica Prize. Divorces Julia Urquidi.
1964   Returns briefly to Peru for a visit to the Amazon jungle.

1966   Publishes *La casa verde (The Green House)*.
1967   Publishes *Los cachorros* ("The Cubs").
        Awarded Rómulo Gallegos Prize.
1968   Residence at Washington State University
        (Pullman, Washington) and in London.
        Publishes a dialogue with Gabriel García
        Márquez, *La novela en America Latina:
        diálogo*.
1969   Publishes *Conversación en La Catedral
        (Conversation in The Cathedral)*. Residence
        in London.
1970   Publishes with Oscar Collazos and Julio
        Cortázar *Literatura en la revolución y rev-
        olución en la literatura*. Residence in Bar-
        celona.
1971   Publishes *García Márquez: historia de un
        deicidio* (García Márquez: Story of a
        Deicide) and *Historia secreta de una novela*
        (Secret History of a Novel). Residence in
        Barcelona and trip to Peru.
1973   Publishes *Pantaleón y las visitadoras
        (Captain Pantoja and the Special Service)*.
        Residence in Barcelona.
1974   Returns to Lima to live there.
1975   Publishes *La orgía perpetua: Flaubert y
        "Madame Bovary"* (The Perpetual Orgy:
        Flaubert and Madame Bovary).
1977   Publishes *La tía Julia y el escribidor (Aunt
        Julia and the Script Writer)*. Named Presi-
        dent of PEN Club International.
1981   Publishes *La guerra del fin del mundo (The
        War of the End of the World)* and *La
        señorita de Tacna (The Missus from Tacna)*.
1983   Publishes *Kathie y el hipopótamo* (Kathie
        and the Hippopotamus) and *Contra viento
        y marea* (Against Wind and Nausea).
1984   Publishes *Historia de Mayta (The Real Life
        of Alejandro Mayta)*.

1

The History of a Passion: Introduction to Mario Vargas Llosa

Mario Vargas Llosa is the prodigy of the writers associated with the "boom" of Latin American literature. With the possible exception of Carlos Fuentes, he has also been the most prolific. By the mid-1970s, this disciplined Peruvian—at that time still not forty years old—had published enough for three respectable lifetime careers. First, he was the renowned creator of five novels; second, he was an academic scholar, author of two critical studies and numerous articles; and third, he was a journalist widely read throughout the Hispanic world.

By 1966, at the age of thirty, Vargas Llosa was already one of the most prominent writers in Latin America. That year he was awarded the Rómulo Gallegos Prize in Caracas, the most prestigious honor a novelist can receive in Latin America. Since then, his international reputation has grown remarkably. Most of his fiction has been translated into English and there have been numerous studies of his work; in the late 1970s he was named President of the International PEN Club; by the 1980s his name has been included in the list of potential candidates for the Nobel Prize.

His story is one of passion and it is a passion for literature. This passion has revealed itself in terms of the
intimate relationships with books that have influenced
him, such as *Madame Bovary*; in the remarkable discipline he has exercised in his writing; and in the rigor he
regularly demonstrates in defending the author's right
to freedom of expression. Vargas Llosa has quoted
Flaubert to explain how writing is "almost a physical
function, a way of being which includes the entire individual."[1]

A personal insight into this passion for life and
literature came to me in the autumn of 1983, when
Vargas Llosa appeared in St. Louis to deliver a lecture.
The highlight of this visit was the trip we took to Hannibal, Missouri, to visit the home of Mark Twain. As
might be expected from a Latin American writer nourished in his youth on American writing, Vargas Llosa
was interested in the original editions of Twain's books
that were on display at the Twain Museum; he was also
fascinated by other nineteenth-century objects from
Twain's life. Upon returning to St. Louis, we met with
a colleague in English, a Twain specialist. Some of
Vargas Llosa's questions about Mark Twain were the
standard queries concerning the American's fiction.
Apparently dissatisfied with what he had learned
about the writer from Hannibal, Vargas Llosa probed
further: "What were Twain's passions? Did he have a
lover?" Such issues are quintessentially those of Vargas
Llosa. The inquiry about Twain's personal life emanated
from Vargas Llosa's conviction that all writers function
as a consequence of passion. The question of lovers
responds to Vargas Llosa's admitted interest in the side
of life that some intellectuals might consider embarrassingly mundane: the lovers and "affairs" that provide the material for soap operas rather than for classic
novels.

Vargas Llosa's Fiction: An Overview

A love affair—and soap operas, in fact—provide the anecdotal material for Vargas Llosa's sixth novel, *Aunt Julia and the Script Writer* (1977). The novel develops two story lines in alternating chapters. The odd-numbered chapters relate the somewhat autobiographical story of a love affair between an adolescent writer-to-be and his aunt, several years his senior; the even-numbered chapters are soap operas produced for Peruvian radio by one of the adolescent's colleagues at a radio station. The writer of the soap operas becomes a Latin American celebrity, and Vargas Llosa fully exploits the humorous potential of the situation. His previous novel, *Captain Pantoja and the Special Service* (1973), was also in a humorous vein, satirizing the Peruvian military. Set in the jungle in northeastern Peru, it tells the story of a fanatic military officer who, when given orders to placate soldiers who are molesting the local girls, organizes institutional prostitution that proves embarrassingly successful.

Aunt Julia and the Script Writer and *Captain Pantoja and the Special Service* are the product of a mature writer confident of his craft. They are also Vargas Llosa's most entertaining books. His more substantive novels are *The Time of the Hero* (1963), *The Green House* (1966), *Conversation in The Cathedral* (1969), and *The War of the End of the World* (1981). In addition, he has published a short novel, *The Cubs* (1967), and, more recently, *Historia de Mayta* (*The Real Life of Alejandro Mayta;* 1984).

The first novel, *The Time of the Hero*, is set in a military school in Lima. The main characters, who are adolescents, represent a cross-section of Peruvian society. They simultaneously propagate and suffer the cruel violence and rituals of daily life in the school. Many of

the boys' adventures seem trivial, merely the antics of
schoolboys. The actions of the cadets, however, expand
to involve them in the broader Peruvian society.[2] The
result is a moral novel.

The use of narrative segments, flashbacks, and
several narrators make *The Time of the Hero* an adventure in technique. In his next novel, *The Green House*,
Vargas Llosa further develops narrative techniques initially explored in the first. The two basic stories of *The
Time of the Hero* (the one in the school and the one in
the city) actually evolved into five identifiable story
lines. *The Green House* expands in physical setting: its
panoramic vision covers two general areas, the Amazon
jungle and the northern coastal area of Peru. Its five
stories are woven into the two settings.

The panoramic vision, various narrative techniques, and story lines become even more complex in
Vargas Llosa's most ambitious novel, *Conversation in
The Cathedral*. Set during the period from approximately the late 1940s to the early 1960s, it encompasses
many aspects of social and political life in Peru during
the dictatorship of Manuel Odría, which lasted from
1948 to 1956. The protagonist, who belongs to Vargas
Llosa's generation — those who experienced the Odría
regime during adolescence and early adulthood —
spends four hours talking with a friend in a bar named
"La Catedral." Waves of dialogue spread out to cover
the entire time span and the broad physical setting of
the novel, which includes Lima and several provinces
of Peru.[3] This challenging work of fiction, which was
originally published in two volumes, involves some six-
ty characters, a subtle montage of dialogue, and a complex manipulation of structure and point of view, as
will be discussed in Chapter 5.

Each of these first three novels is an adventure in reader
participation, requiring one to master Vargas Llosa's

techniques. Obviously, the reading of a novel such as
Conversation in The Cathedral cannot be taken lightly. (As one critic has quipped, however, the author
could respond that he does not undertake the writing
lightly.[4])

Even Vargas Llosa's two humorous novels, which
followed this initial cycle of most demanding fiction,
are not to be dismissed as light entertainment. (Their
serious implications are discussed in Chapter 5.) *The
War of the End of the World* contains elements that can
be associated with much of the previous fiction, and in
this sense may be seen as a synthesis of Vargas Llosa's
writing career. Like *Conversation in The Cathedral*, it
is a monumental production. Its 568 pages represent an
exhaustive research into the history and region of its
setting, northern Brazil at the end of the nineteenth
century. Unlike the early novels, however, it is basically
a straightforward and chronologically narrated account.

The Spanish-American Context

Vargas Llosa had the good fortune of publishing his
first novels during the 1960s, precisely at a moment
when the international reading public began to take
notice of Latin America. He was one of the key figures
in the rise of the contemporary novel there. Along with
Carlos Fuentes, Julio Cortázar, and Gabriel García
Márquez, Vargas Llosa gained international acclaim
during a period that witnessed the publication of such
novels as Fuentes's *The Death of Artemio Cruz* (1962)
and *Change of Skin* (1968), Cortázar's *Hopscotch*
(1963), and García Márquez's stunning and magnifi-
cent *One Hundred Years of Solitude* (1967).

Vargas Llosa belongs to a tradition of Spanish-

American writing, however, that predates this small
selection of fine novels from the 1960s. The "boom" was
only, in fact, the international recognition of relatively
few novelists belonging to a literary culture that had
initiated dramatic changes in Spanish-American fiction
by the 1940s.

A key writer in this reaffirmation of the right of
invention was Jorge Luis Borges, who published his
Ficciones in the 1940s. Other novels that pointed to the
new direction of Spanish-American fiction were: *El Se-
ñor Presidente* (1946), by the Guatemalan Miguel Ángel Asturias; *At the Edge of the Storm* (1947), by the
Mexican Agustín Yáñez; *Adán Buenosayres* (1948), by
the Argentine Leopoldo Marechal; and the Cuban Alejo Carpentier's *The Kingdom of this World* (1949).[5]
Each of these novelists continued writing through the
1950s. Mexico's Juan Rulfo published his classic novel
Pedro Páramo in 1955. By the mid-1950s Vargas Llosa,
Fuentes, and Cortázar were publishing their initial stories, and García Márquez demonstrated lessons in narrative technique—learned primarily from Faulkner—
with his first novel, *Leafstorm* (1955).

Writers of the generations preceding Vargas Llosa—Borges, Asturias, and Carpentier, among others—
were directly involved with the European avant-grade
of the 1920s. All three, in fact, were in Europe during
that period. Spanish-American writers even produced a
few avant-garde novels themselves during the 1920s
and 1930s. Examples are: the Mexicans Arqueles Vela,
who wrote *El café de nadie* (Nobody's Café; 1926), and
Jaime Torres Bodet, author of *Margarita de niebla*
(Marguerite of the Mist; 1927), and the Peruvian
Martín Adán, who published *La casa de cartón* (The
Cardboard House; 1928). The novels of this period that
attracted most readers, however, were the more traditional and tellurian classics: *La vorágine* (*The Vortex*;
1924) by the Colombian José Eustacio Rivera, *Don Se-*

gundo Sombra (1926) by the Argentine Ricardo Guiraldes, and the Venezuelan Rómulo Gallegos's *Doña Barbara* (1929). Simple and at times even simplistic novels, they have been rejected by the contemporary novelists. Vargas Llosa has described them as primitive efforts at novelization.

The Peruvian Context

"All Peruvian writers, in the long run, are defeated persons."[6] This is how Vargas Llosa has characterized the vocation of writing in one of his numerous statements about the formidable difficulties of surviving as a professional writer in Peru. With rare exceptions, the Peruvian potentially interested in literature has become a lawyer or politician by profession, and a writer on weekends.

A tradition of fiction writing in Peru nonetheless exists. The outstanding writers in nineteenth-century Peru were Ricardo Palma (1833–1919), one of Latin America's best traditional storytellers and recreators of local customs, and Clorinda Matto de Turner, a novelist who dedicated her life and writing to denouncing the injustices suffered by the Indians in Peru. Her *Aves sin nido* (Birds without a Nest; 1899) is generally considered a landmark novel in Spanish-American Indianist literature.[7]

Until the 1940s Peruvian writers produced relatively few noteworthy novels compared to the remainder of the Hispanic world. Those published fall squarely within the realist-naturalist tradition: their primary function was denunciation, particularly with respect to the social injustices perpetrated against the native Indian population. The two novelists who dominated the Peruvian literary scene entirely during the 1940s and

1950s were Ciro Alegría (1909–67) and José María Arguedas (1911–69). Both writers were concerned primarily with indigenous themes. Vargas Llosa has delivered lectures and written extensively about Arguedas[8] and has demonstrated a particular empathy for Sebastián Salazar Bondy (1924–65). He has used Salazar Bondy as the example, par excellence, of the devastating effects of attempting to be a professional writer in Peru.[9]

The Peruvian historical context is perhaps even more important for Vargas Llosa's work than the literary tradition. The historical setting of his work stretches over much of the twentieth century.[10] As one critic has aptly pointed out, Vargas Llosa's novels are profoundly discontented visions of Peru.[11] The novelist has explained his vision of his task as a writer in Peru as follows: "Literature in general and the novel in particular are expressions of discontent. Their social usefulness lies principally in the fact that they remind people that the world is *always* wrong, that life should *always* change."[12]

Recent Peruvian history, indeed, provides the novelist with many sources of discontent. Twentieth-century Peru has been characterized by occasional periods of social and economic progress, but instability has been the general rule.

Several types of governments and leaders since World War I have accompanied Peru in its limping journey through recent decades. Throughout the 1920s a U.S.-supported President, Leguía, served primarily the interests of the local oligarchy and foreign investors. Poor economic conditions for the working classes and inflation resulted in the formation of two powerful populist movements. The leftist APRA (Alianza Popular Revolucionaria) was founded in 1924 by Raúl Haya de la Torre as a response to postwar inflation. Another populist leader, Sánchez Cerro, founded the Unión Revolucionaria, right-wing and nationalistic party which, like the APRA, found its main support among the working class. According to Vargas Llosa, in Piura in every home in the working-class neighborhood called La Mangachería (an important setting of *The Green House*) had a picture of its hero, Sánchez Cerro. This hero took power in 1931 only to be assassinated in 1933 — quite likely by a supporter of the APRA. Neither political stability nor economic conditions improved in the 1930s or 1940s.

The government of José Luis Bustamente, a moderate liberal elected in 1945, gave power to Haya de la Torre and the *apristas*, but General Manuel Odría took over the government in 1948 with the backing of the oligarchy, which had become alarmed over the leftist tendencies within the Bustamente government. "With Odría, barbarism reigned once more in Peru," Vargas Llosa has explained.[13] Not only brutal and oppressive, Odría's eight-year regime was corrupt and stultifying. Odría permitted elections in 1956, which resulted in the presidency of Manuel Prado, who was elected with the support of his former enemies, the *apristas*. Near the end of Prado's second term in 1962, elections were held. The three candidates were Odría, Haya de la Torre, and Belaúnde. After a period of political and military maneuvering following the elections, and a brief military junta, Belaúnde was elected. Belaúnde received 39 percent of the vote, Haya de la Torre 34 percent and Odría 26 percent. The setting for *Conversation in The Cathedral* is the regime of Odría and the beginning of the government of Belaúnde.[14] Peruvian novelist Julio Ramón Ribeyro also published a novel on this period, *Cambio de guardia* (Change of the Guard; 1976), a work that had been written several years before it was finally published.

Biographical Overview

"I was convinced that the best thing that could happen to anyone was to be Peruvian."[15] That is Vargas Llosa's recent estimation of how he felt as a ten-year-old returning to his homeland after having spent the first part of his life in Bolivia. He was born in 1936 in Arequipa, a town of moderate size in the coastal southern desert of Peru. His now-estranged mother and grandparents moved to Cochabamba, Bolivia, when he was an infant. During his childhood years Peru became more of a legendary place for Vargas Llosa, one idealized from his readings about the Incas, than it was the nation he would come to know many years later.

Moving to Piura, a town on the coastal desert in northern Peru, when he was ten-years old was only a partial introduction to his country. Piura offered at least as much myth and legend for Vargas Llosa's youthful imagination as it did the social, political, and economic realities. The mature writer has described his experience in the town that would be the setting for *The Green House* as follows: "Piura was a wonderful town full of happenings that sparked the imagination. There was La Mangachería, a district of huts made of reeds and mud, where the best *chicha* (alcoholic cider) taverns were found, and La Gallinacera, the district between the river and the canal."[16]

It was not until a move to Lima that the idealized and legendary Peru of his childhood became the multiethnic and hierarchical society with such vast social inequities, political injustices, and overwhelming problems that would later be portrayed in his fiction. Vargas Llosa's reaction to Lima was unfavorable from the outset: "I went to Lima for the first time when I was just growing out of childhood. I hated the city from the beginning because of the unhappiness I felt there. My parents had been separated and then reconciled after

ten years."[17] This initiation into middle-class Peruvian
society in adolescence was, from his own account, typical: he learned the usual games, music, and dances of
his friends, and experienced the first embarrassing and
painful rituals of adolescent romance.

His true *rite de passage*, and stark revelation about
Peruvian society, would come in 1950, when Vargas
Llosa's father sent the fourteen-year-old boy to a military school. It was perhaps the most significant event of
his first fourteen years, as the author explains:

My father, who had found out I was writing poems, feared
for my future (a poet is doomed to die of hunger) and for my
"manhood" (the belief that poets are homosexual is still very
developed) and to protect me from these dangers he decided
that the perfect antidote was Leoncio Prado Military School.
I spent two years as a boarder at the school, which was a
microcosm of Peruvian society.[18]

It was a society that the young Vargas Llosa so thoroughly deplored that he was allowed to return to Piura
for his last year of high school. But literature excited
him: he was an enthusiastic reader of Hugo and Dumas.[19] Other signs of the emerging writer (aside from
the poems his father had discovered) also became evident. He began working part-time for a newspaper and
wrote what is unquestionably his least-important literary creation, a virtually unknown play entitled *La
huida del Inca* (The Flight of the Inca).

The next period in Vargas Llosa's life, the mid-
1950s in Lima, was extraordinarily difficult. In 1953 he
entered the University of San Marcos, where he studied
for the traditional and stable career of a lawyer. But he
also dedicated himself to his true literary passion, and
held multiple part-time jobs to earn a minimal subsis-
tence. Much of this work was in collaboration with various newspapers and magazines. His situation worsened
when, at the age of nineteen, Vargas Llosa scandalized

his family by wedding his aunt (by marriage), Julia Urquidi. This turbulent period in the author's life would serve as the basic anecdotal material for the novel he would write some two decades later, *Aunt Julia and the Script Writer*. In 1956 and 1957 several of his stories, which were to be collected later in *Los jefes* (The Leaders), began to appear in Peruvian literary supplements and magazines.

In 1958 Vargas Llosa's literary vocation advanced decidedly. The French magazine *Revue Française* declared him the winner of a short-story contest, and sent him to Paris for a month. The French treated him as a guest of honor and even introduced him to one of his heroes, Albert Camus. Within a few months after his return to Lima, he had arranged for a scholarship to write a thesis in Madrid on the Nicaraguan poet Rubén Darío. In reality, the trip to Spain was only a pretext to return to Paris, where he arrived in 1959 with the promise of a scholarship.[20] The scholarship was never forthcoming, and Vargas Llosa soon found himself once again subsisting on a variety of jobs: first, as a Spanish instructor in a Berlitz school and, later, with *France Presse* and French radio and television.

Vargas Llosa virtually became a permanent resident of Paris for a little over a decade and, during the stay, made himself one of Latin America's major writers. There were a few brief trips to Peru, but for the most part he used the period from 1959 to 1969 to write three major novels: *The Time of the Hero*, *The Green House*, and *Conversation in The Cathedral*. He had already written a first version of *The Time of the Hero* in Spain; the labor in France involved writing and rewriting a mammoth 1,500-page manuscript.

The early Paris years were also an exciting period literarily and politically. He read the classics, and, in addition, established friendships and maintained contact with some of Latin America's most respected intellectuals: Carlos Fuentes, Julio Cortázar, Alejo Carpentier, and Jorge Luis Borges, among others. These were also the years of the Cuban Revolution. In two journalistic articles published in 1962 following a visit to Cuba, Vargas Llosa portrays Cuban life in quite favorable terms.[21] But José Miguel Oviedo, Vargas Llosa's most knowledgeable biographer, maintains that the predominant factor in the writer's life during this period was his work. In this respect Vargas Llosa's model at that time was the fanatic disciplinarian of literature, Julio Cortázar.[22]

Publication of the original Spanish manuscript of *The Time of the Hero* was difficult, but international recognition was swift once the novel was finally issued by Seix Barral of Barcelona, the most prestigious publisher of fiction in the Hispanic world. Vargas Llosa has explained how the novel, which exposed the author's vision of the Leoncio Prado Military School, was received in Peru: "The book had a brilliant reception: one thousand copies were ceremoniously burned in the patio of the school and several generals attacked it bitterly. One of them said that the book was the work of a 'degenerate mind,' and another, who was more imaginative, claimed that I had undoubtedly been paid by Ecuador to undermine the prestige of the Peruvian army."[23] Of more significance, however, was the immediate praise of Latin America's most renowned writers and critics, and Vargas Llosa's being awarded two international literary prizes.

Despite his new celebrity, Vargas Llosa's daily routine in Paris remained largely unchanged. Upon the completion of *The Time of the Hero* he had begun the initial drafts of *The Green House*. During the year 1964 he continued writing reviews and articles on Sartre, Hugo, Hemingway, and Simone de Beauvoir. That same year he made a second trip to the Amazon jungle to carry out further research for the novel in progress.

His initial venture, with the Mexican anthropologist
Dr. Juan Comas, had taken place in 1958. Apparently
this introduction to the exotic jungle was as revealing to
him as had been the Leoncio Prado before: it opened
his eyes to an entirely new Peru never before imagined.

By the period of 1965–66 the list of Vargas Llosa's
activities — as well as the list of his publications — become too lengthy to enumerate. He married his second
wife, Patricia Llosa. The increasing number of pieces
for newspapers and magazines included a still revolutionary stance on political issues. In November 1965,
for example, he wrote a "*Toma de posición*" supporting
armed guerrilla warfare in Peru. That same year, he
traveled to Cuba as a judge for the Casa de las Américas literary prizes. Moving from Paris to London in
search of more privacy, he finished the short novel *The
Cubs*. In 1966 *The Green House* appeared in the original Spanish, and *The Time of the Hero* in its English
translation.

The apogee of Vargas Llosa's prominence in the
Hispanic world came in 1967 in the form of his receiving its most prestigious literary prize, the Premio Rómulo Gallegos. At the ceremony for this prize in Caracas, he delivered his much-quoted statement on
literature and revolution: "*La literatura es fuego*" (Literature is fire). Seen in retrospect, however, it is possible to trace a consistent line of thought, from the mid-
1960s to 1971, which demonstrates his change of
position from strict adherence to, and support of, socialist principles and regimes, to dissociation from all
dogmatic and authoritarian governments, including
Marxist.

Such a stance has been considered heresy by many
Latin American intellectuals. But, as early as 1966 Vargas Llosa published articles that began to clarify his
eventual political position. In an article entitled "*Una
insurección permanente*" (A permanent insurrection),

published in March 1966, Vargas Llosa supports the idea of socialism but defends the right to criticize within socialist systems. Here he begins defining his own type of socialism. The following year he penned articles that were vigorously opposed to censorship on both sides of the East–West block. One piece criticized censorship in the Soviet Union and the other was a polemic against censorship in Great Britain.[24] This questioning of Soviet policies in 1967 probably made a split with Castro's Cuba inevitable.

By 1970, lines of direct confrontation between pro-Cuban Hispanic intellectuals and Vargas Llosa were clearly defined. In April 1970 he defended the fiction of the "boom" writers, responding to an ideologically pro-Cuban attack directed at him by the young Colombian intellectual Oscar Collazos.[25] Vargas Llosa openly criticized Fidel Castro by name four months later (August 1970).[26] The definitive rift between the writer and Soviet–Cuban bloc occurred in 1971. As a result of the case of the Cuban poet Heberto Padilla (a celebrated issue in Latin America), Vargas Llosa wrote two open letters to Cuba. The first, addressed to Haydée Santamaría of the Cuban government, expressed Vargas Llosa's unwillingness to make a promised visit to Cuba because of censorship and repression (April 5, 1971). The second was a letter directed to Fidel Castro, signed by numerous Latin American writers, asking Castro to reconsider his most recent actions with respect to intellectuals and indeed make Cuba the "model of socialism" that the leftist intelligentsia had expected. Vargas Llosa still considered himself a supporter of the Cuban Revolution; some distance has nevertheless remained between him and other Latin American writers who unequivocally defend all the policies of Castro and other nations aligned with the Soviet Union.

In addition to the heated political debate, the late 1960s and early 1970s were years that highlighted Var-

gas Llosa's extraordinary artistic and scholarly discipline. He wrote two of his most lengthy texts, *Conversation in The Cathedral* (1969) and the study of García
Márquez's fiction, *Gabriel García Márquez: historia de
un deicidio* (Gabriel García Márquez: History of a Deicide; 1971). The original Spanish edition of the novel
was published in two volumes. Although this work contributed to his prestige as a novelist, it probably did
little to broaden his readership. His study of García
Márquez — an exhaustive 667-page analysis of the Colombian's complete fiction — is still one of the best
source books on that writer; it is almost as interesting
for its revelations on Vargas Llosa as for those on its
subject.

After the publication of the novel *Captain Pantoja
and the Special Service* and more essays during the year
1973, Vargas Llosa returned to Peru in 1974. He
noticed those changes that had occurred since he left at
the age of twenty-two, and another of his passions
came forth in his description of the return:

I left Europe and didn't live in my country again for any
length of time until 1974. I was 22 years old when I left and
38 when I returned. In many ways, I was a totally different
person when I came back. But as far as my relationship to my
country is concerned, I think it has not changed since my
adolescence. It is a relationship that can be defined with the
help of metaphors rather than concepts. Peru is for me a kind
of incurable disease, and my feeling for her is intense, bitter,
and full of the violence that characterizes passion.[27]

Despite the mixed feelings, Vargas Llosa has basically remained in Peru, with his second wife, Patricia,
since 1974. During this period he has dedicated himself
to the type of activity and writing that had characterized his previous career. He wrote three more novels,
Aunt Julia and the Script Writer, *The War of the End
of the World*, and *The Real Life of Alejandro Mayta*; his

essays have appeared regularly throughout the Hispanic world—including a book-length study of Flaubert's *Madame Bovary* titled *La orgía perpetua: Flaubert y "Madame Bovary"* (The perpetual orgy: Flaubert and *Madame Bovary*; 1975). His newspaper pieces on political issues have been consistent with his earlier writing: he regularly speaks out against any type of censorship or repression of rights of the artist. Being named President of PEN Club International in the late 1970s gave him an international forum in which to discuss such issues. By the mid-1980s, Vargas Llosa was established as one of the world's major writers. His novels, which are translated into numerous languages (as are his scholarly essays and incisive political writings) have made him one of the most respected writers of the twentieth century.

2

The Beginnings:
The Early Stories (1959)
and *The Time of*
the Hero (1963)

Vargas Llosa's early short stories unquestionably figure
as his secondary fiction. With respect to aesthetic quality, many of them should be classified as good amateur
writing at best. His first novel, however, *The Time of
the Hero*, published only four years after these relatively innocent stories, is among the most sophisticated
works of contemporary fiction.

"The six stories from 'The Leaders' [*Los jefes*] are
a handful of survivors out of the many I wrote and tore
up between 1953 and 1957, while I was still a student
in Lima," Vargas Llosa writes. "I have a certain fond-
ness for them, because they remind me of those difficult years when, even though literature mattered more
to me than anything else in the world, it never entered
my mind that one day I would be a writer — in the real
sense of that word."[1]

Even the reader unaware of the difficult years of
which Vargas Llosa speaks will perhaps be conscious of
other types of problems, those also related to an
apprenticeship in the craft of fiction. With the publica-

tion of *The Time of the Hero* in 1963 the situation
concerning the art of storytelling has been reversed: the
novel is an adventure in narrative technique comparable in this sense to the writings of such masters as
Faulkner (whom Vargas Llosa had been reading) or
Pynchon, who was also embarking on his career. These
early years mark an astonishing development in Vargas
Llosa's writing.

The First Stories

When Vargas Llosa was writing his first stories, he says,
he "read Faulkner, but . . . imitated Hemingway."[2]
Hemingway's style — the sparse language of journal-
ism — is evident in several of the six stories of *Los jefes*.
The adventure-filled plots of some of these stories recall
Hemingway and the American Western movies that
Vargas Llosa enthusiastically viewed in Lima. The
writer also admits to an echo of Malraux's *L'Espoir*,
which he was reading while writing the title story for
the original Spanish volume, *Los jefes*. (It is important
for the reader of the English translation to realize that
it differs from the Spanish volume.)[3]

The collection contains two general types of stories, each of which was subsequently developed in his
later fiction. There are the stories that deal with moral
dilemmas in their social context and those that are less
concerned with copying an objective social reality than
what is often called "romance," or the creation of a
mythical fictional world.

"The Leaders" is a story in the first category. It
portrays a conflict at a school between students and
school authorities. Its twenty-five pages are divided into five parts, which develop the plot in a dramatic
fashion. The narrator within the story and his group of

friends rebel against school authorities over a disagreement about the final examination schedule. The matter
of the examinations functions in the story as a pretext —
a technical pretext for Vargas Llosa and a thematic one
for the characters. The basic conflict is established in
Part I. The students view the scheduling of the examination as entirely unfair. The school officials defend
this decision with tired clichés about God, discipline,
and the supreme values of the spirit. By the end of Part
II, the group decides to rebel. Having established this
basic plot, Vargas Llosa delves into the substance of the
story in the second part.

The moral issue then acquires new shades of
meaning when it is viewed from strictly the students'
point of view. The youths leave school and confront the
issues among one another. At the beginning of the second part the narrator questions the real substance of
the moral problem for the youths:

Could the rallying cry have reached every grade? I didn't
want to torment my brain again with pessimistic assumptions, but I had my eye on Lou a few feet away from my desk,
and I felt anxious and doubtful, because deep down I knew
that what was at stake was not the exam schedule, not even a
question of honor, but a personal vendetta. Why give up this
lucky chance to attack the enemy when he'd dropped his
guard?[4]

In effect, the boys avoid the moral correctness of their
acts: the narrator-protagonist's side predominates in a
physical confrontation, and consequently they agree to
use the same examination schedule of previous years.

In the third part the setting is again within the
school, where the boys approach the director. The narrator is part of the group and thus by implication is in
tacit agreement with their leader, Lou, when he questions the justice of the school's operation. But the protagonist is equally as disgusted with Lou as he is with

the principal. The narrative structure reaches a turning point in Part IV. The conflict is articulated once
again via a confrontation among the youths. Once
again Lou's voice predominates, and the boys agree to
boycott classes. The students overcome Lou physically
and end the boycott by entering the school. At the conclusion Lou confronts the narrator and his friends,
questioning why they abandoned the strike. The two
settle the issue with another fight. But the narrator
shakes hands with Lou, and the story ends as follows:
"I felt an arm on my shoulder. It was Javier."

The meaning of "The Leaders" changes significantly with the denouement, particularly with the final lines. Vargas Llosa portrays a very human and significant moment during the maturation process of two
boys. The reader senses that the narrator has matured
when he shakes hands with someone with whom he
bitterly disagrees, instead of resorting, as before, to
physical force. A firm sense of affirmation is manifest
in the final two lines with the image of an arm on a
shoulder, and these sentences mark the understatement
and brevity that were trademarks of the Hemingway
influence on Vargas Llosa.

In addition to the types of moral issues to be elaborated extensively in *The Time of the Hero*, this short
story also announces the structure of the early novels.
The initial sections of the story alternate between the
school setting (focus on the conflict between authorities
and the students) and the group setting (focus on the
real issue at hand, the conflict between the two boys).
Parts I and III take place in the school and II and IV
outside. (This pattern will be exploited in a vastly more
complex form in *The Time of the Hero*.) The fifth part
of the story is a fusion of the locations, just as the two
issues — the moral one and personal one — are resolved
together in the story's final lines. Language is also im-
pressively well controlled here for a beginning writer:

Vargas Llosa resists the temptation to editorialize. The paucity of words and the suggestive quality of the final lines also betray an adolescent writer.

Three of the early stories—"The Challenge" (*El desafío*), "A Visitor" (*Un visitante*), and "The Grandfather" (*El abuelo*)—are less related to an immediate social reality than to the fictional tradition of romance. They represent Vargas Llosa's early flirtation with romance.

In "The Challenge" Vargas Llosa transforms a fight between two men into something more than a conflict between two specific individuals: it has the universal overtones of myth. This story involves a confrontation in which pure physical brutality predominates over characterization or moralizing. For several pages the reader experiences an abstract movement of bodies in ritual combat. Several factors contribute to the notion of a ritual: the fact that the reader is not informed exactly why the two men are fighting; the darkness and vagueness of the physical setting; and the ritualistic movements of the two combatants. With respect to this last element, the narrator describes the movements of one fighter as a dance and the entire scene as a magical spectacle.

"The Challenge," like "A Visitor" and "The Grandfather," lays the groundwork for the later creation of myth in *The Green House*. "A Visitor," in fact, can be conceived by the reader as an anecdote that could be incorporated into *The Green House* with relative ease: the style, setting, and even some of the characters will actually appear later in the novel. The style creates an exotic ambience from the first sentence: "The sands lap the front of the inn and come to an end there: from the hole serving as a door or from among the reeds, the view slides over a white, languid surface until it meets the sky." This sentence moves the reader's eye from the sand to the sky, offering a progressively broader vision.

The evocation of this image of the sand and white desert creates a fictional universe closer to myth than empirical reality. This broad vision and poetic discourse are similar to certain descriptive passages in *The Green House*.

The initial sentences of this story also contain a quality of mystery. The grass "hides" everything in the terrain. One can see a "hint" of a wood thicket, which seems to be only the suggestion of a much more extensive and forbidding forest. (In the original Spanish this second "forest" is really a "jungle" [*selva*], which is even more exotic.) The anecdote on which "A Visitor" is based tells another story of a vendetta: a black, named Jamaican, arrives at a home and molests a woman whose husband is absent. Soldiers eventually take Jamaican from the home, freeing the woman. The story ends with the group of soldiers riding off with the woman, abandoning the intruder in the forest to die. The exotic scene of the opening paragraph was not gratuitous: the threat suggested at the beginning is fulfilled in the ending.

During this early period, Vargas Llosa was concerned with the social realities of Peru and the responsibilities of the writer who feels *engagé*. Pure imagination and invention, however, are the predominant characteristics of "The Challenge" and "A Visitor." The third story of this type, "The Grandfather," tells of an old man who systematically plans an evening of terror for his grandson. The story is relatively powerless because both the plans and their execution fail to evoke mystery and terror in the reader. Thematic and technical elements of the story do appear, however, which relate to Vargas Llosa's later writing.

The author begins by using specific narrative techniques to create a subjective experience for the reader. As in the first paragraph of "A Visitor," the story opens with an exotic and potentially mysterious setting:

"Each time a twig cracked or a frog croaked or the window panes rattled in the kitchen at the back of the garden, the old man jumped spryly from his improvised seat on a flat rock and spied anxiously through the foliage. But the boy still had not appeared."

The narrator plunges the reader into a situation that will not be clarified until later: placed among plants and animals, the reader knows only that the old man is anxiously spying on someone. The first two paragraphs are dedicated primarily to the creation of this rarefied atmosphere. With a shift to the past the reader learns of the events that immediately preceded this evening. The grandfather, Don Eulogio, had found a skull on the outskirts of town. Upon discovering it, his imagination is triggered: " . . . [he] amused himself immensely, imagining that the thing was alive" (p. 71). The entire episode is generated by an act of the imagination, which Don Eulogio attempts to carry out in the series of events that follows. At the end the boy sees the skull with a candle and is terrified. He runs away screaming. Having enjoyed the pleasure of this terror, Don Eulogio walks away smiling and content. Obviously Vargas Llosa's primary interest in this story is the creation of a patently exotic anecdote. The young writer, however, fails to create the immediate experience of the fantastic for the reader.

The two remaining stories in the volume — "On Sunday" (*Día domingo*) and "The Younger Brother" (*El hermano menor*) — like "The Leaders," are more related to situations in social contexts. "On Sunday" is a story of growing up. An adolescent, Miguel, faces three tests of manhood. The first occurs when he declares his love to Flora. When rejected by her, he feels defeated at the hands of his rival, Rubén. This situation sets up two other tests.

Miguel challenges Rubén to a beer-drinking contest before their peers, but loses. His final challenge is

swimming in the sea. This time Miguel wins, primarily
because Rubén suffers a stomach cramp. During the
swim, the boy's motivation for winning is revenge. A
key point in the story, consequently, is the moment
when Miguel overcomes the personal vendetta: when
Rubén is drowning, Miguel saves him. Just as important is his behavior at the conclusion, when the two
competitors arrive at the beach where their friends
await them. Rubén admits his loss, but claims that he
could have won had they competed in a swimming
pool. Miguel says nothing of this statement nor of his
having saved Rubén's life. His silence is the first act
of any of the youths to surpass adolescent bravado. Paradoxically, Miguel does not appear to be conscious-
ly aware of his true accomplishment; that is, not
the swimming stamina, but the importance of his silence.

The final sentence, "A golden future was opening
before him," is an irony to the elevated importance the
narrator has accorded Miguel's physical challenge. As
such, this sentence is more a reflection of what the boy
thinks than an accurate prediction of the future direction of his life. The reader can appreciate the humor
involved with Miguel's ingenuousness. A possible second level of irony appears: there could be some truth in
the possibility of Miguel's "golden future," but not, as
he believes, because of his swimming victory. Rather,
his future seems enhanced by the admirableness of his
silence on the beach in a moment when he could have
boasted.

"The Younger Brother" deals with a moral question. Two brothers, David and Juan, search for an Indian who has escaped from their ranch. Their sister
claims to have been molested by the Indian, and the
brothers intend to kill him. The story focuses on Juan's
concern with the moral issue of the murder. At the
beginning of the story David ridicules Juan's preoccupation over what is for himself a routine and seemingly

insignificant act. Juan's consternation is also evident during their trip back home after the murder. When the sister later reveals that her accusation against the Indian was a lie, Juan expresses his feelings with a physical outburst: he rides off on a wild horse to free the remaining Indian prisoners.

The young writer is obviously concerned with the moral questions surrounding the issues of social injustice and racism. In ideological terms, the story can be seen as an expression of the conflict between the dominant classes and the Indian population in Peru or in Latin America in general. The communication between the two brothers is the most visibly articulated version of the collective antagonistic discourses of social classes: David's language is that of the dominant landowners and Juan's incorporates some of the Indians'. The narrator's language is also dialectic, involving a process of interaction between different types of languages.

The text of "The Younger Brother" has occasional echoes of a Sartrean existentialism, which stress man's ultimate responsibility: mankind is connected in a tight network in which each individual is responsible for his or her actions, and these actions affect not only the individual involved but also others. The sister's lie — the first act of what Sartre would call *mauvaise foi* — is not only an immoral act, but also sets in motion a series of other acts with moral consequences: the hunt, the moral speculation on Juan's part, the murder, the sister's attempt to save the Indian before the end, and Juan's final series of actions. Sartrean language is functional in describing key events in the story and also operates as its catalyst. Vargas Llosa employs, too, some of the language of American films, as the author himself has suggested: "'The Younger Brother' lapses into indigenist themes, flavored, perhaps, with motives originating in another of my passions of that period: Hollywood Westerns."[5]

The six stories of this early period offer two basic
models with respect to narrative point of view. "The
Leaders" and "The Challenge" involve a narrator within the story and the remaining four stories feature
omniscient narrators. Two additional factors are worth
noting. First, as one theorist of fiction has pointed out,
ideology is not just a matter of thematic content
"poured into" a text, but is the very fabric of textual
organization.[6] On the basis of this observation it can be
understood that analysis of narrative point of view in
these six stories and later novels is not exclusively a
matter of describing formal characteristics of texts. It is
more important to consider how point of view interacts
with content and shapes the reader's experience. Second, there are significant variations of point of view in
these six texts, even within the two basic models
described above.

The narrators in "The Leaders" and "The Challenge" operate similarly but with slightly different
roles. In "The Leaders" the first-person narrator functions as a protagonist who occasionally reveals his
thoughts and feelings during the development of the
story. As both witness and central participant to the
events at hand—the conflict between students and
school authorities—he provides both an exterior and
interior view. The exterior view, which narrates actions
of the authorities and other cadets, stresses the social
conflict. (Were this same anecdote related by a narrator
outside the story, it could have been a fiction of social
conflict with possible moral overtones.) Certain reactions on the part of the narrator render a very person-
alized narration: " . . . but I had my eye on Lou a few
feet away from my desk, and I felt anxious and doubtful . . . " (p. 49). Later he describes his feelings as follows: "I felt a thin, hot thread coursing along my
tongue and that calmed me" (p. 54). Each of the sentences, and the final lines of the story, make "The

Leaders" a successful characterization of an individual
and this person's maturation. "The Challenge," in contrast, features a narrator who is a witness to events
rather than a protagonist. His physical and temporal
distance from the events narrated make the encounter
between two men a universal rather than a particular
account.

The third-person narrators in the four other stories
also vary in their function and effects. In "The Grandfather" the narrator communicates the thoughts and
feelings of the grandfather as he plots against the boy.
It is one of the least successful stories of the volume
since the narrator does not examine the boy psychologically, nor does he successfully create an experience of
terror for the reader, as already noted.

"A Visitor" renders an entirely different type of experience. The narrator tells the story in a present time
that fosters a sense of immediacy: "Now Dona Mercedi-
tas dozes, lying across two socks. A little farther away,
the goat pokes his nose in the sand, stubbornly chews a
splinter of wood or bleats in the cool afternoon air.
Suddenly, it picks up its ears and freezes. The woman
half opens her eyes" (pp. 76–77). The use of the present
tense, the detail of the descriptions, and the imagery
that the narrator employs frequently in this story contribute to the reader's direct experience of the conflict.

"On Sunday" and "The Younger Brother" are both
stories related in the past tense. The narrator in "On
Sunday" provides interiorizations of Miguel and thus
focuses on his feelings as he experiences key moments of
his youth. "The Younger Brother" includes occasional
interiorizations of Juan, but the narrator's position is
fundamentally exterior to the characters, providing actions and dialogue. Consequently, the moral implications of the story are not vitiated by personal feelings:
the reader observes a social situation with a distance

that allows for moral judgment. A comparison of the
narrative situation in "On Sunday" and "The Younger
Brother" provides an appropriate example of how ideology is part of the very fabric of textual organization:
the difference in thematic content cannot be isolated
from the reader's experience as determined by the narrator's position.

The language is not unitary in this volume of six
stories from Vargas Llosa's apprenticeship years. The
language does reveal Vargas Llosa's self-admitted imitation of Hemingway. In addition, however, it also
demonstrates more of the Faulkner whom he was reading than even Vargas Llosa apparently has realized: the
experimentation with the subtleties of narrative point
of view is more like that of Faulkner than of Hemingway. The many-languaged discourse — or heteroglossia — of the volume also includes the language of Sartre,
of American Western movies, and of Peruvian indigenous literature.[7] Vargas Llosa begins to develop the two
basic modes of fiction that will be evidenced in his
novels of the 1960s: "The Challenge," "A Visitor," and
"The Grandfather" point to the tradition of romance,
whereas "The Leaders," "On Sunday," and "The Younger Brother" deal with moral issues and social contexts
that will be novelized in later works such as *The Time
of the Hero.*

The Time of the Hero

One critic writing in the mid-1960s described *The
Time of the Hero* as a moral novel.[8] This critic views
Vargas Llosa as a cynic who fails to propose an alterna-
tive to the painful and sordid reality presented. Rather,
the only hope offered in *The Time of the Hero* is
through the individual's own moral conscience.[9] José

Miguel Oviedo, who maintains that this novel is the one most concretely based in Peruvian reality, suggests that the constant moral questioning places in doubt any type of social determinism.[10] Indeed, the plot and structure make inevitable an awareness of Peruvian society and a judgment of the characters' actions.

The Time of the Hero consists of eighty-one narrative segments that appear in two parts and an epilogue. Each of the two parts contains eight chapters and these chapters generally consist of four or five narrative segments. One chapter has only one narrative segment, two chapters have ten narrative segments, and the epilogue and three other chapters contain three narrative segments. This complex structure also features a variety of narrators within and outside the story. Approximately one-third of the novel consists of first-person narrations — thirty-six of the eighty-one segments.[11]

The action that places the novel in movement is the theft of a chemistry examination by Cava, a student in the Leoncio Prado Military School. Unable to identify the culprit of this robbery, the school authorities confine all the cadets to the barracks indefinitely. After suffering confinement for several weeks, and consequently unable to visit his girlfriend on the weekend, one of the cadets, nicknamed Slave (Ricardo Arana), reveals the thief's identity to the school officials in exchange for the right to leave the premises. The school subsequently expels Cava.

Jaguar, the aggressive leader of the youths in the school, along with his peers, suspects that someone has betrayed them. Soon thereafter, Slave is shot during some military maneuvers. Even though Jaguar appears to be guilty of the crime, the school officials conclude that the death is accidental, caused by Slave's own rifle. Slave's only friend, Alberto, is aware of the animosity Jaguar held toward Slave and tells the officials of the murder. Those in the upper echelon of the school hierarchy prefer to conceal the scandal that would inevitably follow a revelation of the facts. Alberto had written pornographic stories to sell to his peers; school officials use their knowledge of this to blackmail him into silence. The one officer who seemed morally capable of questioning the situation, Gamboa, finds his career prospects ruined when he is sent to an isolated post in the provinces. An epilogue tells of the main characters' lives and careers after leaving the military school.

The intricate pattern of plot development and the different temporal and spatial planes of reality make even an understanding of the series of events and relationships among characters a challenging intellectual experience. Hardly a better novel could be found to exemplify Meir Sternberg's proposition that suspense and plot development are essential to fiction and should not be overlooked in preoccupation with more "highbrow" concerns.[12] In *The Time of the Hero* two structures are developed in parallel fashion. One involves a series of details related to character and plot; the second is the development of the novel in broader terms.

Included within the first structure is a narrator. In the first half of the novel a series of narrative segments appear regularly that are related by an unidentified narrator. The fifth narrative segment of the first chapter is one such section: the reader experiences the sounds and words of the youth's perverse sexual acts, but the narrative filter is unidentified. This identity is only a minor issue: the reader's experience would not be radically altered by knowing who narrates. Nevertheless, as the novel progresses the reader's curiosity is piqued. The question is answered at the beginning of the second half of the novel, when the narrator states: "When they started calling me Boa . . . "[13] With these words Boa resolves some of the most persistent of the relatively minor problems.

Similarly, the second narrative segment of the first chapter creates questions concerning identities when it describes the arrival of "Richi" or "Ricardito" to a new neighborhood, Magdalena Nueva. It soon becomes apparent that these narrative segments are describing Slave's childhood before he began attending the Leoncio Prado. By the third chapter, such flashback narratives dealing with Slave (and also Alberto) are no longer enigmatic, but another question surfaces: Who is the narrator of the first section, which deals with Tere and is related by a narrator within the story? The reader logically attempts to relate this section to Slave or perhaps even Alberto, since they are characters associated with Tere during the novel's "present." Later it will become apparent that these anecdotes, in fact, tell of Jaguar's relationship with Tere, but before his entrance into the Leoncio Prado.

These minor perplexities are an important factor in maintaining reader involvement in the first half of the novel. By the second half, most of such questions have been resolved and more thematic matters become central. The military exercise that ends Part I is just a game of sorts, but a change takes place when Jaguar kills Slave: the potential death that terminates Part I moves the novel to another plane of thematic importance. The problems of Part II are of adults in real social contexts, not of adolescent games. In the second half, moral issues become the substance of the novel.

The central problem for the reader in the second half of the novel is how those involved will confront Slave's murder. The reality of the adolescents in Part I was one of instinctive cruelty and sordidness; the reality of the adults in Part II is calculated manipulation of human lives.

The Time of the Hero presents itself to the reader as a box of secrets. The minor and major questions involve both a moral questioning and a puzzle to be solved. The cadets' internal world is also one of secrets: it is one cadet's failure to keep a secret, after all, that is the main catalyst in the novel's action. In this way Vargas Llosa develops a parallel between theme, structure, and the reader's experience: all are predicated on the issue of secrecy and solving the enigmas created by secrecy.

A significant factor in the reader's experience is the author's use of a variety of narrators. The twenty-six first-person narrations and remaining third-person narrations are not uniform in their revelation of either the interior psychological realities of the characters or the presentation of exterior social reality. Critics of *The Time of the Hero* have correctly viewed its fictional world as a microcosm of Peruvian society. The novel portrays an unjust hierarchical society in which all social relations operate on the basis of dominance or coercion. The value of the text as a denunciation of certain characteristics of Peruvian and Latin American society, however, should not obscure the fact that the use of narrative point of view and other subjectifying factors are essential to the total experience.

The novel features three narrators who function also as characters within the story: Alberto, Boa, and Jaguar. Alberto's narration is particularly important because of his central role in the novel. His narrative segments are also a combination of the two basic modes of both first and third person. Alberto's first segment, which appears in the third section of the first chapter, reads as follows:

I could go and tell him I've got to have twenty *soles*, but I know what'd happen, he'd get all weepy and he'd give me forty or fifty, but that'd be just like telling him I forgive you for what you've done to my mother and you can keep on whoring around all you want as long as you give me good bribes. Alberto's lips were moving silently under the wool muffler his mother had given him a few months before (p. 14).

These two sentences, which are only the first two of an extensive one-and-a-half-page paragraph, contain three types of discourse. Each is systematically synthesized in this paragraph and throughout the novel. The first type of discourse is Alberto's standard interior monologue, which begins with the first "I" and continues through the words "telling him." The remainder of this sentence ("I forgive you . . . ") is, in effect, a type of indirect monologue which could have been placed within quotation marks. The third type of discourse is the narration, next, by an omniscient narrator outside the story who describes Alberto.[14] The reader's perception of the situation in this first paragraph, then, is determined by a relationship between three types of discourse: one which is ostensibly thought, a second that is ostensibly spoken, and a third that is ostensibly written and literary. (They are "ostensibly" so since, technically speaking, all three are *written discourse*.) In this sense Vargas Llosa employs heteroglossia in this bit of text.

This presentation of Alberto renders him someone whom the reader constantly judges: the dialogues between characters and between discourses make Alberto a complex character and reveal his inconsistencies. (In a 1976 article Sharon Magnarelli demonstrated these inconsistencies and his tendency to lie.[15]) Even though Alberto is sexually inexperienced, he writes pornographic literature. For example, the omniscient narrator observes the following about Alberto's stories concerning the prostitute Golden Toes and other sexual experiences: "Alberto talked about Golden Toes as much as anyone else in the section. No one suspected that he knew about Huatica Street and its environs only by hearing, because he repeated anecdotes he had been told and invented all kinds of lurid stories" (pp. 108–9). Later, Alberto deceives Slave's parents by telling them how highly all the cadets regarded their son (p. 211). When Alberto denounces Jaguar, even he is not absolutely certain of this claim (p. 302). Alberto's reliability is constantly placed in question, and his double presentation by the omniscient narrator and by himself as narrator supports this duplicity.

The second narrator within the story, Boa Valdivieso, employs language that is considerably different from Alberto's. He narrates thirteen segments of the novel. Alberto, "The Poet," has a facility with a language; Boa is capable of only minimal verbal expression and directs his discourse to a dog, Skimpy. He tends to offer visceral reactions to the situations at the Leoncio Prado. The sections he narrates are interior monologues without the duplicity of the two narrators in many of Alberto's segments. The reader sees him as the buyer of Alberto's pornographic novels, and as the one who defended Jaguar. Boa is revealed primarily, however, by his own narrative.

Like Alberto and many characters in this novel, Boa is not what he appears to be initially.[16] His brutish nature, worship of machismo, and racism are his most salient characteristics. He openly admits to bestiality, the sexual assault of a cadet, and deliberately breaking the leg of his dog. Boa admires Jaguar's exhibitions of machismo and deprecates his French teacher for effeminate weeping. His racism is apparent in his comments about both the *cholos* (Indian and Caucasian mix) and the Indian boys who have mountain-peasant backgrounds. What makes Boa interesting as a character, however, is the reader's dual perception of him: his physical abuse of animals and persons is contrasted with moments of affection for his pet and absolute loyalty to his friends.

The structure and narrative point of view of *The*

Time of the Hero are effective vehicles for both creating the world of the Leoncio Prado Military School and inviting the reader to participate actively in this act of creation. Neither this type of structure nor use of point of view is, in itself, an innovation. Critics have already pointed out Vargas Llosa's technical predecessors, among them Dos Passos and Faulkner. At the end of this novel, however, the Peruvian writer pioneers a technique of telescoping time that he exploited more fully in his next two novels. In a conversation between Skinny Higueras and Jaguar, for example, the dialogue moves immediately to a previous conversation between Teresa and Jaguar, with no written indicator of the temporal jump:

> "I told her everything," Jaguar said.
>
> "What's everything?" Skinny Higueras asked. "That you came looking for me with a face like a whipped dog? That you turned into a thief and a whoremonger?"
>
> "Yes," Jaguar said. "I told her about all the robberies, at least the ones I remembered. I told her about everything except the presents, but she guessed right off."
>
> "It was you," Teresa said. "All those packages. You sent them to me."
>
> "Ah!" Skinny Higueras said. "You spent half your earnings in the whorehouse and the other half sending her presents. What a character!" (p. 404).

The first three quotations — the interchange between Skinny Higueras and Jaguar — take place in a recent past. Higueras and Jaguar discuss an incident involving Teresa. Vargas Llosa intercalates a previous conversation, in the more distant past, between Teresa and Jaguar: When Teresa says, "It was you," she is speaking in this distant past, even though there is no indicator of the change in time frame. It is a technique that provides for the reader's direct participation in the events presented. The reader of Vargas Llosa's novels makes adjustments in the reading process to understand these passages, temporarily suspending traditional assumptions about how dialogue works.

This initial telescoping of dialogue at the end of *The Time of the Hero* is just a first step in the formation of the ideal "Vargas Llosa–reader." Narrative techniques such as this, specific to Vargas Llosa's fiction, will be more fully exploited in the next two full-length novels, *The Green House* and *Conversation in The Cathedral*.

3

Maturity:
The Green House (1965)
and *The Cubs* (1967)

The narrative techniques of *The Time of the Hero* contribute to its suspense and its effectiveness in telling the stories of several characters. The demands placed upon the reader in this first novel are multiplied in the fiction published during the remainder of the 1960s, but for those readers who respond to these demands, this is unquestionably the most exciting period of Vargas Llosa's writing.

Two of Vargas Llosa's most knowledgeable readers, José Miguel Oviedo and George McMurray, consider *The Green House* superior to the first novel.[1] Oviedo maintains that it is a more notable work because of its innovation in narrative technique and its deep penetration of Peruvian reality. McMurray claims that *The Green House* surpasses the first novel in scope, technical skill, and imagination. According to Vargas Llosa, this complex novel with its many intertwining stories represented a type of "emancipation" from a variety of experiences of different periods of his life.[2]

Like most novelists, Vargas Llosa has eschewed any extensive analytical or critical commentary about his own work. His literary essays deal with books other

than his own. He has been willing, however, to discuss
the personal experiences and settings, and even touches
upon discourse that could be considered statements of
intention. Furthermore, in effect Vargas Llosa's overall
writing codifies intentions in a way that the books of a
writer who publishes only fiction cannot.[3] This codification is an important element in the fictionalization of
an "ideal reader." Vargas Llosa has written an essay
that the reader of *The Green House* can use to gain
valuable insights into the personal experiences and Peruvian reality which, according to the author, were the
basis for the creation of that novel. This essay, published in Spanish as *Historia secreta de una novela* (Secret History of a Novel), explains many of the actual
places, situations, and characters that appear in this
novel.

Secret History of a Novel

In this seventy-five-page essay Vargas Llosa surpasses
what could easily have been an anecdotal catalogue of
information about remote areas of Peru. In discussing
the arduous process of, and motives involved in, writing *The Green House* (from 1962 to 1965), the author
has explained it in this essay as follows: "It was during
that period that I realized that novels are written primarily with obsessions and not convictions, that the
contribution of the irrational was at least as important
as the rational in the making of a fiction."[4]

Vargas Llosa begins his "secret history" by explaining the background to the two locations of the novel,
Piura in northern Peru and Santa María de Nieva in the
jungle. They represent two totally different historical,
social, and geographical worlds. For the author, Piura
represents civilization: it is the desert, the color yellow,

cotton, and Spanish Peru. Santa María de Nieva is the jungle, vegetal exuberance, the color green, tribes that have not yet entered into the flow of Western history, and institutions and customs that seem to be leftovers from the Middle Ages and the Stone Age.

The Green House originated, according to this essay, in 1945, when Vargas Llosa's family arrived in Piura the first time. They lived there for only a year. The writer claims, however, that the things he did, and the people and places with which he became acquainted, remained so firmly imprinted in his memory that no other period in his life left such an impression.

One of the images he would remember from Piura was of a mysterious green building on the outskirts of town that held a special fascination for him as a youngster. There was something malign and ambiguous about it. It became lively at night and was only visited by men. The place that Vargas Llosa even then called "the green house" was, of course, a brothel. The other vivid image was of the Mangachería, a working-class and *lumpenproletariat* neighborhood with its own very special character. The people in the Mangachería lived in shacks, but they were proud of its music, bars, food, and other traditions. It had a vital popular culture. Inhabitants of the Mangachería were also proud adherents to General Sánchez Cerro, a conservative leader with fascist tendencies. According to popular legend in Piura, Sánchez Cerro was born in the Mangachería.

In 1946, Vargas Llosa moved from Piura with his family and did not return until 1952. Both "the green house" and the Mangachería were still there. When he entered "the green house" for the first time, he found it less elegant than he had remembered and imagined it before. Nevertheless, it was still quaint and, in his own words, "truly original."

In 1957, on the way to Spain, he became acquainted with a town in the Amazon jungle in Peru,

Santa María de Nieva, the second main setting for *The Green House*. This visit, according to Vargas Llosa, was a moving experience, which revealed a totally new nation: "I discovered a face of my country that was totally unknown by me; I think that until then the jungle was a world which I only had a feel for from reading Tarzan and certain movies." He discovered a Peru of the Middle Ages and the Peru of isolated Indian tribes. There Vargas Llosa saw how Indians were actually captured by government soldiers and turned over to Catholic missions to be taught Christianity and become "civilized." Once they were "civilized," paradoxically, they had no place in either their own former tribes, whose customs they had learned to despise, or in white and mestizo Peruvian society. They would usually be sent to government officials or merchants, destined to be maids or to hold menial jobs. Those who successfully traveled to Lima would be, at best, cooks or, at worst, prostitutes in the "green houses" of the capital.

Vargas Llosa also learned of the business dealings of the jungle. He met an Aguaruna Indian chief named Jum — the same name that will appear in the novel. Jum had been tortured and humiliated by government soldiers because he had organized the Indians' rubber commerce in a way that circumvented profits by the (white) middle men.

Another important character in *The Green House*, Fushía, was a legend of the jungle whom Vargas Llosa never met but about whom everyone spoke. He was a Japanese merchant who had installed a type of feudal kingdom in the jungle — terrorizing the local Indian tribes and exploiting them for their rubber and other merchandise. The case of this particular real-life jungle figure offers a notable example of the peculiar symbiosis between social reality and literary invention: Fushía's name is confused in both Vargas Llosa's personal experience and in the novel. The name of this legendary Japanese chieftain was Tushía. During the writing process, Vargas Llosa explains in his "secret history," the "T" of his name was converted into an "F" and the real "Tushía" became a fictional Fushía. Tellingly enough, the characters in the novel eventually confuse his name in the same fashion. Near the end of the third part of *The Green House*, a lieutenant searching for Fushía asks, "What's his name? Tushía? Fushía?"[5] Soon thereafter, the lieutenant asks " . . . where had that Tushía hidden?, everything in due time, or Fushía, where was he?" (p. 249).

The author's personal experience in both Piura and the Amazon enrich the fiction that has resulted from it. A reader can also benefit from a basic knowledge of the geographical setting, as well as the Mangachería. In addition to Vargas Llosa's own informational essay and codification of his intentions, his critics have uncovered further background to *The Green House*.[6]

The Green House

Whatever one's interest or awareness of northern Peru and the Amazon jungle may be, the central issue is Vargas Llosa's transformation of this anecdotal material into a novel. The text consists of four parts and an epilogue, each of which is preceded by a section that could be considered a prologue (although it is not identified as such in the text). Parts I, III, and the epilogue contain four chapters; Parts II and IV have three. The chapters of Parts I and II contain five narrative segments; those in Parts III and IV have four narrative segments. The novel in Parts I through IV, then, consists of sixty-three narrative segments, which are generally four to six pages in length.

One critic, appropriately enough, has likened the plot of *The Green House*, and its uncanny unfolding, to the fluvial webs in the Amazon with its maze of main rivers, tributaries, and small streams, now joining unexpectedly, now virtually disappearing in the thick undergrowth.[7] Despite the weaving of its many stories, the novel offers two broad settings that correspond to two general plots.

In the first setting, Piura, a young man named Anselmo arrives and, after becoming well acquainted with Piura's inhabitants and ways of life, builds the Green House in the desert on the outskirts of the town. Despite the protests of Father García, the new brothel flourishes. Anselmo kidnaps a blind orphan girl, Antonia, and keeps her in the house, where he fathers the child that causes Antonia's death in childbirth. The outraged Father García and the women of Piura burn down the Green House. Eventually a second Green House appears in the city proper. Chunga, Anselmo's daughter by Antonia, is the owner of this night bar. The old Anselmo plays in an orchestra there regularly. From the Mangachería a group called the "Champs," which includes Sergeant Lituma, frequents Chunga's bar regularly. Lituma challenges a friend, Seminario, to a game of Russian roulette and the latter's death results in Lituma's incarceration. His wife, Bonifacia, is seduced by one of the Champs and eventually works in Chunga's Green House as a prostitute.

The second setting and main plot, seemingly unrelated to the first, involves the story of indigenous tribes, merchants, government officials, and missionaries in the area of Santa María de Nieva in the Amazon. Government soldiers bring young Indian girls to the nuns for education at a mission in Santa María. The governor, Reátegui, operates a profitable business by trading for rubber and other goods at a very favorable rate of

exchange and then selling the goods in the city of
Iquitos. Reátegui tortures the Indian chief Jum for attempting to sell his own goods. A voice that narrates
stories related to all these events on the Amazon is that
of Fushía. He tells his friend Aquilino of all his opera-
tions and the key events of his life.

The connection between the two settings of *The
Green House* is provided by the presence of Lituma as a
soldier in the Amazon and his marriage to Bonifacia,
who first appeared in the jungle when she was a young
Indian girl in the mission in Santa María de Nieva. This
overview of the novel's plot in a general sense suggests
obvious parallels with Vargas Llosa's anecdotes of his
"secret history." His artistic elaboration of the story,
however, makes the experience of the novel radically
more different than a brief résumé of the plot might
suggest.

The author has explained the temporal ordering of
the novel as follows: "There is no linear order. I have
tried to render all of these worlds — so opposite, so different — as a totality."[8] A brief overview of the beginning of Part I will provide some idea of how the novel is
constructed.

The prologue to Part I, some twelve pages in
length, is located in the jungle. An omniscient narrator
outside the story tells of soldiers searching for Aguaruna Indian girls to capture for the nuns. The first
chapter consists of five narrative segments. The first
segment (pp. 18–22) takes place at the nuns' mission at
Santa María de Nieva. Sister Angelina and the other
nuns are outraged with Bonifacia because she has allowed the other Indian girls to escape. Fushía begins to
tell his story to Aquilino in the second narrative segment (pp. 22–25); he relates his escape from Brazil by
breaking out of a jail and then continuing to Manaos
and finally Iquitos, in Peru. The third narrative seg-

ment (pp. 22–28) introduces the reader to Piura, offering a panoramic view of its different neighborhoods: the Mangachería, Castilla, Gallinacera, Malecón, and the Plaza de Armas. Corporal Roberto Delgado, Captain Quiroga, and Captain Nieves appear in the fourth segment (pp. 28–31), which is once again set in the Amazon jungle. The fifth narrative segment (pp. 31–34) deals with Lituma's group of friends, the Champs, in Piura. Chapters 2, 3, and 4 of Part I offer the identical five stories, which appear in the same order described above in each of the chapters.

The first five segments present the reader with both ambiguities and outright confusion. Upon the completion of these initial thirty-four pages, the reader is utterly incapable of relating the five narrative segments to one another. There are some initial clues — and also some red herrings. The narrator does note in the first narrative segment in the jungle, for example, that the Sergeant is from the Mangachería. This is the first association that the reader can make between the story in the jungle and the story of Piura in the third narrative segment, which also mentions the Mangachería. The astute reader will also be able to observe a similarity between the third narrative segment and the fifth: the Green House is mentioned once at the end of the third segment and the Champs go there at the end of the fifth. There are also false clues. For example, the first segment deals with the girls' escape and the following segment begins with Aquilino asking Fushía to explain how he escaped (p. 22). The reader searching for relationships between these two contiguous segments will attempt to relate the two escapes. In reality, they are totally unrelated anecdotes.

The five interwoven stories of these different narrative segments cover a period of approximately forty years. They are discontinuous, however, in both time

and space. Michael Moody, in a perceptive analysis of
the novel's structure, has made the following observation concerning the reader's experience with respect to
the development of the multiple stories: the reader observes the concurrent advance of all the plots, which
produces a continual overlapping of temporal levels so
that characters and events are simultaneously viewed
from various perspectives and at different distances in
time.[9] Despite the discontinuities and false clues, the
overlapping advancement of the plot does allow for a
gradual understanding of the overall picture. By the
end of Part I the reader has established the basic system
of the five narrative segments and is able to relate the
jungle story to Piura's story: Wildflower of Piura is revealed, by then, as the Bonifacia of the jungle; the Sergeant of the jungle has been identified as Lituma of Piura.

The logic of cause and effect in a sequential story
line is systematically undermined in *The Green House*.
As Moody has aptly noted, incidents leading to the development of conflicts as well as those pertaining to
their resolution are revealed *before* the exposition of a
climactic moment for each character.[10] For example,
Bonifacia's story at the mission in Santa María de Nieva
has not yet been fully developed when it is revealed that
she has become a prostitute in Piura. The experience is
controlled by the fact that several of the displaced key
events occur near the end of the novel. The reader does
not see Anselmo take Antonia to the Green House, for
example, until Part IV. Lituma also leaves Santa María
de Nieva with Bonifacia in Part IV. In the very last
segment of the novel Dr. Zevallos tells the dramatic
story of Chunga's birth and Antonia's death.

This complex pattern of relationships in itself determines the reader's perception of the characters as
human beings. They tend to lose their individual identity and exist, rather, as elements within the overall

scheme. Moody has appropriately pointed out that crucial acts in the lives of the characters define them not so much in terms of their own personalities as in terms of their relationships to their surrounding world.[11]

Characterization in *The Green House* is achieved by distinct narrative techniques for character portrayal that provide a resultant wide variety of fictional entities. The techniques portray many characters in an "exterior" fashion that reveals only words and actions; other characters are revealed psychologically. As persons they range from simple one-dimensional figures to sophisticated individuals. Anselmo is the most complex and probably most fascinating character in the novel.

Vargas Llosa's method of presenting Anselmo changes as the novel progresses. The initial segments of Part I introduce him in a strictly exterior fashion. By the conclusion, however, the reader is privy to the most intimate thoughts as they are revealed in interior monologues.[12] At the beginning of the novel the exterior presentation of Anselmo makes him an enigmatic figure. Both the reader and the inhabitants of Piura view him as a mystery since neither he, nor the narrator, reveals his past or his motives for coming to Piura. He seems superior to the people of the town. Given his special status there and his enigmatic nature, he becomes a mythical figure for the reader as well as for the inhabitants of Piura. At the end of Part I, the narrator explains Anselmo's mythical status in Piura as follows:

New myths about Don Anselmo arose in Piura. According to some, he took secret trips to Lima, where he kept his money and was buying property. According to others, he was only the front man for a business group that had the Chief of Police, the Mayor, and several ranchers among its members. In popular fantasy, Don Anselmo's past became enriched, sublime or bloody deeds were daily added to his biography (p. 90).

Anselmo embodies several characteristics of the archetypal hero: he was reared in a far country; his childhood is undisclosed; he arrives in what will be his future "kingdom"; he became a hero through the performance of miraculous feats that demonstrated his power over the elements. (Moody proposes other characteristics that relate him to the archetypal hero.[13]) Nevertheless, a more appropriate description of Anselmo's characterization is that of "mythologizing" rather than true mythmaking. There are individual details that make him into a myth, particularly in Part I, but by the end of the novel he is totally humanized.[14]

A set of contradictory factors surround the characterization of Fushía. At the beginning of the novel the story that he tells of his escape from jail in Brazil makes the reader question his integrity—he betrays two friends in order to flee safely. His treatment of other persons, particularly the Indians in the Amazon, makes his character even more dubious. Because Fushía is also the victim of political and economic circumstances beyond his control, however, his own vulnerability inspires compassion.[15] Fushía prospered during the war, trafficking contraband rubber in collaboration with Julio Reátegui. But he spends the rest of his life struggling after Reátegui's betrayal leaves him with no legal business and few resources for survival. The temporal framework of his appearance in the novel makes him, too, a mythical character. The time and space of his story are basically indeterminate. Fushía's voyage at the end of his life toward an inevitable death gives his being the special resonance of a prototype.[16]

The highly dialogic content of the novel makes characterization a process of evaluation on the part of the reader. One particular technique Vargas Llosa uses for these indirect characterizations is "choral" characters who are largely unindividuated.[17] Lituma and Bonifacia, for example, are presented in Part III

through what could be called the chorus of the Champs
and the chorus of the "orchestra." The musicians' account of the encounter between Lituma and Seminario
is a blending of the three musicians' distinct impres-
sions of the incident: one offers verbal recollections,
another a vivid visual summary, and the third emotional reaction.[18]

Vargas Llosa's use of narrative point of view and
related techniques are also effective devices for characterization. The narrator's presentation of the narrative
segments dealing with Piura illustrates a more subtle
control of narrative point of view. The initial Piura
segment (pp. 25–28) portrays the town from a distant
point of view. The segment begins as follows: "As it
crosses the dune region, the wind that comes down off
the Andes heats up and stiffens: reinforced with sand,
it follows the course of the river, and when it gets to the
city it can be seen floating between the earth and the
sky like a dazzling layor of armor." The reader's eye
follows, across the town, in the remainder of the paragraph as the narrator mentions several neighborhoods.

The presentation is strictly exterior. In addition to
what the narrator presents visually, he recounts what is
said about the town: "The night is full of stories in
Piura. The peasants talk about ghosts; in their corner,
as they cook, the women gossip and discuss misfor-
tunes" (p. 26). The narrator relates several anecdotes of
"what is said" in and about the town. Despite the narrator's panoramic vision of Piura and seemingly classic
position of omniscience outside the story, he is not totally omniscient in the Piura segments. For example, he
makes the following observation about the "stranger"
(Anselmo): "In the reddish light of dawn, as the sun
tongues snaked their way out across the desert, the
stranger *must have been* happy to see the first cactus
plants, the singed carob trees, the white houses of Cas-

tilla . . ." (my emphasis, p. 44). The narrator, like any observer, conjectures about how the character "must have" felt.

In the remainder of the segments the narrator takes a position as an insider of Piura who does not examine Anselmo psychologically or even know more about his background than the inhabitants of Piura. The effect of this precise position of limited omniscience on the part of the narrator is to make Anselmo as mysterious and potentially legendary a character for the reader as he is for the citizens of the town. An extreme contrast then appears in Anselmo's characterization in Part IV: the only extensive interior monologues of the novel are three of Anselmo's interiorizations dealing with his relationship with Antonia. The character who was presented with systematic distance in Part I becomes the one with whom the reader is most intimately acquainted by the end.

The outstanding narrative techniques that Vargas Llosa develops specifically in *The Green House* involve innovative uses of dialogue. The telescoped dialogues pioneered at the end of *The Time of the Hero* (see Chapter 2) become more complex and considerably more frequent in *The Green House*. The following dialogue appears in the first Fushía segment of the novel:

"But you already told me about that when we left 1
the island, Fushía," Aquilino said. "I want to hear 2
how you escaped." 3
"With this picklock," Chango said. "Iricuo made it 4
from a wire on his cot. We tried it out and it can open 5
the door without any noise. You want to see, Jappy?" 6
he said to Fushía. 7
Chango was the older one, he was in for drugs or 8
something, and he was good to Fushía. Iricuo, on the 9
other hand, was always making fun of him. A slippery 10
guy who had swindled a lot of people with a story 11

about an inheritance. He was the one who made plans.   12

"And it happened just like that, Fushía?" Aquilino   13
asked.   14

"Just like that," Iricuo said (p. 23).   15

The dialogues take place on two temporal levels.
Aquilino's initial statement and final question here
(lines 1–3 and 13–14) take place in an immediate past
in the conversation between Fushía and Aquilino. The
dialogue between Chango and Iricuo seems to flow logically with the Fushía–Aquilino conversation, but in
reality it takes place in a past previous to the Fushía–
Aquilino dialogue when Fushía escaped from imprison-
ment in Brazil. Telescoping appears regularly in
the Fushía segments and occasionally in other narrative segments. This technique has two effects. On the
one hand, the use of actual dialogue from the past —
rather than a character's observation of it — makes the
reader's experience with even the remote past direct.
Unlike novels that present some anecdotes directly and
others as indirect experience, *The Green House*
presents the reader with a constant and direct confrontation with multiple planes of reality. On the other
hand, this technique of telescoping dialogues creates juxtapositions of an occasionally contradictory and
paradoxical nature: the reader experiences a capricious reality that seems to be perpetually relative to
circumstances and the subjectivity of the individual
speaking.

Vargas Llosa employs a similar but not identical
technique by intercalating flashbacks into dialogues. In
the third chapter of Part I, for example, the first narrative segment (pp. 55–59) presents alternate views of a
situation by this intercalation. In the dialogue the
Mother Superior questions Bonifacia about the circumstances leading to the Indian girls' escape. The narrator
relates the dialogue as a past event ("said"). The six

flashbacks that illustrate Bonifacia's explanations, however, are in the *present* tense: "Bonifacia claps her hands and the pupils' whispering diminishes but does not stop . . ." (p. 55). The effect of these unorthodox "flashbacks" into a "present" is, like the telescoped dialogues, to create a sense of immediacy for the reader. This particular narrative segment, then, features both an immediate past and an immediate present.

Vargas Llosa uses a diversity of styles to achieve a broad range of effects. Many traditional forms of written language, such as the traditional sentence and paragraph structure, are vastly elaborated into new forms. The controlling, omniscient narrator occasionally describes the physical setting in a language wrought with images. Metaphorical language suggests the atmospheres of Piura and the jungle, respectively; these scenes are compelling not because of any particularly innovative techniques, but by means of a thoroughly traditional use of suggestive language. The author's handling of the scene in which Fushía and Aquilino depart for the last time is revealing:

He [Aquilino] murmurs and keeps on withdrawing, now he is on the path. There are puddles in the low spots, and a very strong breath of vegetation invades the atmosphere, a smell of sap, resin, and germinating plants. The old man continues withdrawing, the small pile of living and bloody flesh is still motionless in the distance, it appears behind the ferns. Aquilino turns around, he runs toward the cabins, Fushía, he would be back next year, whispering, he should not be sad. It is raining very hard now (pp. 346–47).

This is Fushía's death scene. We note, however, that the death is only suggested by momentarily portraying Fushía as a motionless object. Of the five sentences, three focus on human beings (the first, third, and fourth) and the other two focus on nature. In this passage and throughout the book, Vargas Llosa equates physical nature and humans by means of a language that emphasizes neither: both nature and persons are portrayed by means of only brief exterior descriptions. The last line of this passage is also quite suggestive. The limpid pile of flesh would seem to be beaten down by the rain. Although he is no longer present, Fushía dies in the last line.

In this jungle setting and throughout the novel descriptive passages of any length are very rare. Rather, Vargas Llosa fixes an impression with a single image.[19] For example, the images of Fushía's death and of the Green House in the desert at the edge of Piura are permanently associated with the novel. Such images also offer brief glimpses of the Indian world, as Moody has pointed out: "Gradually, the reader assembles a picture of naked, dark flesh tattooed with unknown symbols, of yellow teeth filed down to points, of murky eyes that shine inhumanly in the dark, and of stealthy movements by creatures who vanish before their presence is fully registered. This alien world is so charged with animal quality that even the Indian dwellings acquire the appearance of wild beasts . . ."[20]

Closely related to style is the many-languaged text of heteroglossia that is woven into the dialogues. There are two languages that pervade all communication in this novel: the language of Christianity and the language of the Mangachería. The language of Christianity emanates from two focal points, the mission in Santa María de Nieva and Father García in Piura. Bonifacia's entire story, in a way, is a story of learning the language of Christianity. In the Amazon region there is a constant tension between this language of Christianity and other discourse, such as the language of commerce and government. Government officials carefully adopt this language of Christianity when they negotiate with the nuns to take the girls from the mission to the outside

world. Even the conversations between Fushía and
Aquilino, although often vulgar, vacillate between the
language of the sacred and the profane. In Piura, Father García's zealous articulation of Christian language—screamed from his pulpit and even in the
streets—is in direct conflict with the numerous other
discourses of Piura.

The language of the Mangachería, like that of
Christianity, has multiple and ubiquitous manifesta-
tions. Just as the language of Christianity is expressed
with the emotion of screams and songs in churches, the
language of the Mangachería is sung regularly by the
Champs in their theme song: "They were the champs,
work wasn't for them, they lived off the rest, they wig-
gled their asses, and now they were ready to empty
their glasses." (The song in the original Spanish is more
vulgar.[21]) Their language is one of machismo. They
speak constantly about seducing females and demon-
strating their masculine prowess before other males.
Lituma's roulette confrontation with Seminario is,
above all, an act of machismo. The language of the
mangaches even has its peculiar idiomatic forms in the
Spanish.[22]

By the end of the novel the two dominant languages are visibly moribund. Bonifacia has forgotten
much of the Christian language she had learned in Santa María de Nieva. Father García's tired language has
not only lost its forcefulness, but is being replaced by
the foreign discourses of modernity: technology and
science are part of the world of the movies that the
youth prefer over Mass at church. The theme song of
the Champs has also lost its vitality by the end and
there is a general sense that their language will soon be
forgotten; the Mangachería will be destroyed for the
construction of new buildings.

The Green House is a denunciation of Peru's basic
institutions. The denuncation is emphasized by the fact

that in each prologue section an indigenous group or
individual Indian is abused or victimized. In the prologue to Part I the soldiers attack and capture Aguaruna girls. The Mother Superior gives two Indians to
Governer Reátegui and Don Fabio to begin Part II. The
prologue to Part III features Jum, who is outraged because of the humiliating torture he has suffered.
Fushía, Pantacha, and Nieves attack and loot an Indian
village. The repetitive cycle of abuse of Indians culminates with the epilogue in which Governer Reátegui,
the nuns, and Corporal Delgado discuss the punish-
ment that will be inflicted upon Jum. The perpetrators
of abuse and the particular individuals victimized
change throughout the book, but the pattern remains
the same. The coordinated exploitation controlled by
the triangular relationship between the government,
the military, and the church is the classic Latin American model.

The dialogue among the Champs in the Mangachería represents the confluence of the ignorant language of machismo and the extreme-right politics of
their hero, Sánchez Cerro. In one conversation among
the Champs, for example, they follow a discussion of
Lituma's machismo ("You were a he-man, buddy")
with the following affirmation: "We all belong to the
Unión Revolucionaria here in Mangachería. Faithful
followers of General Sánchez Cerro, right down to the
bottom of our hearts" (p. 71).

The confluence of the cult of personality and
political and religious discourse has been another traditional pattern in Latin American societies. A statement
that an average man in Piura — a taxi driver — makes to
Dr. Zevallos after Anselmo's death is revealing. The taxi
driver praises Anselmo by means of a language of both
politics and religion: "The *Mangaches* are going to be
very sad, boss," the driver says. "The harp player was
like a god to them, even more popular than Sánchez

Cerro. Now they'll light candles for Don Anselmo too, and pray to him the way they do to Domitila, the holy woman" (p. 363).

In *The Green House* Vargas Llosa develops a form of fiction with which he initially experimented in some of his initial stories: romance. In creating characters with mythical qualities — Anselmo and Fushía — he moves toward a romancelike fiction. The qualities of the romance have been defined by one critic as follows: ". . . being less committed to the immediate rendition of reality than the novel, the romance will more freely veer toward the mythic, allegorical and symbolist forms."[23] The story of Anselmo, his Green House, and his love for Antonia, as well as the story of the distant and decrepit Fushía, describe "what never happened nor is likely to happen" — another definition of romance.[24] Vargas Llosa has achieved in *The Green House* an effective synthesis of not only two general plots, but also of two traditional forms of fiction: the novel and the romance.[25] This flirtation with romance was not coincidental. Vargas Llosa has written about the Spanish novels of chivalry — the original Hispanic version of romance — as his most cherished works of literature. He has even written a preface to an edition of one of these novels of chivalry (see Chapter 7).

The Green House is a patently dialogic novel in ways more complex than even M. Bakhtin could have imagined when he coined the term heteroglossia. First, it is richly dialogic in its incorporation of multiple layers by means of telescoping. The novel is also dialogic in its use of many-layered discourses from different spheres, such as religion and the varied social classes. The reader is in constant contact with a reality in continual flux. Since the variant communications of languages are in opposition, reality takes on a capricious quality, that the reader becomes accustomed to questioning.[26] Reality becomes so innately relative, in fact, that the nature of truth and the possibility of truth are called into question. And this type of questioning — of the techniques specific to *The Green House* — is essential to the experience of the Mario Vargas Llosa reader, who also comes to question the possibility of attaining a complete understanding exclusively through rational means.

"The Cubs"

Although the novelette "The Cubs" exhibits virtually none of the technical complexity of *The Time of the Hero* and *The Green House*, it did present a technical challenge to the author. Vargas Llosa wanted to tell a boy's story, but the problem was who would tell it.[27] He found the answer in the *barrio*. But:

How to ensure that the collective narrator didn't drown out the various voices speaking for themselves? Bit by bit, filling up my wastebasket with torn sheets of paper, that choral voice gradually took shape, dissolving into individual voices and coming together again in one that gives expression to the entire group. I wanted "The Cubs" to be a story more sung than told and, therefore, each syllable was chosen as much for musical as for narrative reasons. I don't know why, but I felt in this case that the verisimilitude depended on the reader's having the impression of listening, not reading, that the story should get to him through his ears.[28]

There are limits, of course, to how much a text written for musical reasons can offer the same experience in translation. Obviously the syllables chosen for the original Spanish cannot always be reproduced in English. What does indeed function quite similarly in the English version is the "choral voice." The boy's story is told by a plural "we," which represents a small group of his classmates.

The original Spanish edition of "The Cubs" — "*Los cachorros*" — has another special feature, unknown to readers of the English edition. The recreation of the boy's crisis in the 1950s is accompanied by large black-and-white photos of typical scenes of adolescent life in that period, replete with the white socks, tight-fitting slacks, dances and beach parties. The pictures create a nostalgic tone, even though the story itself is not predominantly nostalgic. They also suggest a certain verisimilitude that goes beyond the fact that the story was indeed based on a real event, according to the author: "It [the story] had been going through my mind ever since I had read in a newspaper about a dog's emasculating a newborn child in the Andes. From then on I dreamed of a story about this strange wound that, in contrast to others, time would open rather than close."[29]

The result was a forty-three-page story that relates a boy's tragic life from preadolescence to early adulthood. (The original Spanish edition of the novelette, with the aforementioned pictures and the large print of a children's book is 105 pages long.) The story, divided into six parts, relates the changes in psyche and personality of a young boy who has been emasculated by a dog. The protagonist, Cuéllar, is enrolled in the Champagnat Academy in Lima. In Part I, Cuéllar is presented as the ideal student: his friends pardon his being a disciplined scholar ("grade grubber") because he is a "good pal" with peers and not overly solicitous with his teachers. He also wins his friends' admiration by becoming the school's best soccer player.

A Great Dane breaks into the boys' locker room one day after soccer practice; the others escape, but the dog seriously wounds Cuéllar. Nevertheless, his recovery is speedy, and, by Part II, he reinstates himself as one of the most accomplished players on the soccer team. At school he is now treated with extraordinary care by both teachers and administrators; his wealthy

father had threatened to close down the school after
Cuéllar's accident. The boys soon begin to show their
first interest in girls, learning to dance and to smoke
cigarettes. Cuéllar's psychological problems begin to
surface in Part III. Whereas the other boys begin to
date girls, he becomes progressively more isolated, despite the peer pressure to pursue the opposite sex. His
behavior also becomes erratic: "As days passed, Cuéllar
became more standoffish with the girls, more tight-
lipped and distant. Crazier too: he ruined Kitty's birthday party throwing a string of firecrackers through the
window . . ." (p. 23). By the end of Part III, Cuéllar
and the group graduate from high school.

Cuéllar, now a young adult, demonstrates still
more deviant behavior in Parts IV through VI. He fails
in his only attempt to establish a relationship with a
girl. Now twenty-one years old and still supported by
his family, he regresses to social relationships with teen-
agers, and frequents lower-class bars and dives. In one
of his reckless automobile races, Cuéllar dies in an accident.

Vargas Llosa's most effective device for involving
the reader in this story is the creation of a first-person-
plural "we" narrator. Consequently, the story vacillates
between an insider's and an outsider's view of Cuéllar's
actions. The story begins as follows: "They were still
wearing short pants that year, we weren't smoking yet,
they preferred soccer to all the other sports and we were
learning to surf . . ." To the extent that Cuéllar's acts
are part of those of the group, the "we" narrator provides an insider's view. Since the narrator cannot penetrate Cuéllar psychologically, or describe in detail his
activities away from the group, the vision is that of an
outsider. This intimate awareness of the group setting,
yet exterior and distanced acquaintance with Cuéllar,
makes the reader's experience in understanding Cuéllar

similar to the experience of those characters who are his peers. For both the reader and Cuéllar's peers the precise details of the incident with the dog and many of the other events in Cuéllar's life and, finally, of his death remain ambiguous.

In several ways thematic content and textual organization are tightly bound in this text. As Julio Ortega has observed, Cuéllar's life and behavior are defined primarily by his relationships with others.[30] Narrative point of view, at the same time, is a game of we/they and we/he relationships. The structure also reveals a highly systematic plan of organization, whereby the last two parts are significantly shorter than the others. In this way the text telescopes time, and reflects a common human perception that the older one becomes, the more rapidly time seems to pass.[31] Part VI, which is only three pages long, less than half the length of the other five parts, suggests in its very length Cuéllar's relative unimportance to the group. The acceleration of the pace emphasizes his growing alienation, to the point of total isolation.[32] Consequently, his death is communicated to the reader almost as a footnote rather than as an event central to the story.

Language, in itself, contributes to the reader's understanding of the protagonist and his group. Adolescent speech is reproduced in the original Spanish by the regular use of diminutive forms.[33] The final paragraph reads as follows in Spanish:

Eran hombres hechos y derechos ya y teníamos todos mujer, carro, hijos que estudiaban en el Champagnat, la Inmaculada o el Santa María, y se estaban construyendo una *casita* para el verano en Ancón, Santa Rosa o las playas del Sur, comenzábamos a engordar y a tener canas, *barriguitas*, cuerpos blandos, a usar anteojos para leer, a sentir malestares después de comer y de beber y aparecían ya en sus pieles algunas *pequitas*, ciertas *arruguitas*.[34] (My emphasis.)

They were mature and settled men by now and we all had a
wife, car, children who studied at Champagnat, Immaculate
Conception, or Santa María, and they were building themselves a little summerhouse in Ancón, Santa Rosa, or the
beaches in the south, and we began to get fat and to have
gray hair, potbellies, soft bodies, to wear reading glasses, to
feel uneasy after eating and drinking and age spots already
showed up on their skin as well as certain wrinkles (p. 43).

The four diminutives in the above Spanish — *casita*
(little house), *barriguitas* (little bellies), *pequitas* (little
spots), and *arruguitas* (little wrinkles) — cannot be
translated well into this text. Vargas Llosa has reproduced the language of a particular group, and literally
concludes the story (the last word) with the language
that has been established by the text itself. It is a story
about a boy's inability to integrate himself into an adult
world. The linguistic conclusion to the story is identical
to the fabula's denouement: both the protagonist and
the language remain in a state of perpetual immaturity.

In "The Cubs" Vargas Llosa successfully fabricates
the "sung" novel that he claims to have intended to
write. The group of voices and the regular appearance
of the diminutives achieve this objective. By 1967,
Vargas Llosa's fiction was a mature art which, in fact,
seemed to possess no limits. *The Green House* and "The
Cubs," indeed, represent for his readers a broad range
of writing styles, techniques, and experiences. Seen
within the context of Vargas Llosa's total fiction, however, "The Cubs" is a relatively insignificant predeces-
sor to a far more ambitious "spoken" novel, *Conversation in The Cathedral*.

4

Peruvian Epic: *Conversation in The Cathedral* (1969)

Conversation in The Cathedral may be best described as an epic. Such traditional genre definitions prove inadequate for many contemporary novels, but this is particularly the case in Vargas Llosa's hybrid and complex fictions. The vastness of this novel, however, which seems to encompass virtually all aspects of Peruvian social life over an entire generation during the 1950s, brings to mind the epic. Within the context of Vargas Llosa's work, at least, it is his Peruvian epic. *Conversation in The Cathedral* has also been described as a political novel. As such, it is the story of the Odría dictatorship from 1948 to 1956. Vargas Llosa has spoken of novels which, "despite political themes, are not political novels," and maintains that he aspired to write such a novel with *Conversation in The Cathedral*.[1]

Like García Márquez's *One Hundred Years of Solitude* and Fuentes's *Terra Nostra*, *Conversation in The Cathedral* also seems to be that impossible "total novel" much spoken about by Latin American writers and critics. Vargas Llosa announces this "totalizing" project with an epigram by Balzac: "*Il faut avoir fouillé toute la vie sociale pour être un vrai romancier, vu que le roman est l'histoire privée des nations.*" The totality of Peru fictionalized — which does indeed seem to be

"*toute la vie sociale*" — portrays a corrupt and decadent
nation.

A resounding question set forth by the protagonist
in the second sentence of the novel reads as follows: "At
what precise moment had Peru fucked itself up?" ("*¿En
qué momento se había jodido el Perú?*") This question
will resonate and reappear throughout the text. It can
be associated with three of the novel's most fundamental characteristics. The first, suggested by the phrase
"at what precise moment," points to the importance of
time; whereas in *The Green House* space takes priority
over time, in *Conversation in The Cathedral* time takes
priority over space.[2] The second important element is
Peru itself: the novel will be a portrayal and questioning of an entire nation during a specific historical period. One critic has appropriately called Peru the "obsessive" subject of the book.[3] The third significant
characteristic is suggested by the question mark at the
end of the sentence (or, in the case of the original Spanish, the question marks at the beginning and end). The
novel presents itself initially as a question to be solved.
The reader's task will involve attempting to solve a series of mysteries about character, plot and, indeed,
what happened to Peru and when.

Critical Overview

Vargas Llosa began to explore heretofore unknown terrain when he decided to write what was already being
defined as a "political" novel before its original publication in Spanish in 1969. In addition, he was con-
fronted with the task of creating his fictional material
from real models that were not just a single institution
(as in *The Time of the Hero*) or an anonymous brothel
(as in *The Green House*), but an entire nation.

José Miguel Oviedo has pointed out the author's interest in documentation — creating the real and historical.[4] Vargas Llosa went so far with his documentation that he read Odría's speeches and a security law which his government had instituted in 1949. In 1967, when the novel was approximately half written, he interviewed individuals who had survived Odría's regime. Nevertheless, only one historical event appears directly in the book: the strike in Peru's southern town of Arequipa, in Part III. Oviedo, like many other critics of Latin American literature, has emphasized the predominance of invention over the historical, or of imagination over the mimetic, in *Conversation in The Cathedral*. He states: "His objective is always invention: of characters, of stories, of appropriate forms and styles."[5]

Critics aware of Vargas Llosa's previous work have discussed *Conversation in The Cathedral* as an elaboration and culmination of *The Time of the Hero* and *The Green House*. Mary Davis, for example, asserts that "*Conversation in The Cathedral* reveals the intensification and elaboration of all the characteristic elements of Vargas Llosa's style. No longer do the separations of city and jungle, desert and towns that enliven it matter; everything exists simultaneously."[6] Similarly, another critic views this novel as the epitome of Vargas Llosa's "totalization impulse."[7]

A common topic of discussion has been the "determinist," or "fatalist," vision several readers have ascribed to the 1969 novel. Luis Harss, generally critical of Vargas Llosa's work, considers his writing excessively "determinist."[8] Oviedo has been more defensive of what he has identified as a "fatalistic" vision.[9] Wolfgang A. Luchting has systematically documented the constant failure to which Vargas Llosa's characters are subjected.[10] Such failures reduce all action to a limited number of alternatives and make any type of success unlikely.[11] This type of commentary can place in doubt any possi-

bility of change in the social structures, even though
Vargas Llosa, like many contemporary Latin American
writers, has been an outspoken proponent of social
change. His response has been that what his characters
suffer is the result of a precise historical moment, and
should not be interpreted as a general statement on the
human condition.[12]

Several critics have analyzed *Conversation in The
Cathedral* within the context of other works of world
literature. Vargas Llosa himself has written of his passion for novels of chivalry, especially Martorell's *Tirant
lo Blanc*. Both the writer and many of his critics have
referred to the influences of Flaubert and Faulkner in
all of Vargas Llosa's fiction. Critics have also related
the writer to Balzac, Zola, Pérez Galdós, Tolstoy, Dickens, Joyce, Kafka, Dumas, Melville, Malraux, Henry
James, Beckett, Sartre, and Alfred Döblin.[13]

For Alan Cheuse one of the most outstanding
characteristics of Vargas Llosa's work in general and of
Conversation in The Cathedral in particular is its "har-
dy strain of naturalism."[14] Santiago Zavala's opening
interrogation—"At what precise moment had Peru
fucked itself up?"—is, according to Cheuse, naturalistic both in diction and ethos. The critic also points out
that the opening sequence, which creates a parallel between an epidemic of rabid dogs and the deterioriza-
tion of the psychic lives of the city's inhabitants, further
establishes the novel's roots in the naturalistic tradition.
Nevertheless, Cheuse does admit to a fundamental difference between Vargas Llosa's fictional world and that
of the nineteenth-century naturalists: in *Conversation
in The Cathedral* the manipulation of "environment" is
clearly different from the conventional naturalists who
conceived of the temporal progression of events and
cause-and-effect relationships on characters and actions. It is a book, Cheuse points out, which stands in

the tradition of the great nineteenth-century novelists at the same time that it upsets the reader's "customary notions of naturalism, realism, and fantasy."[15]

Jean Franco carries out a detailed and perceptive analysis of *Conversation in The Cathedral* by comparing it to Albert Camus's *The Fall*.[16] Her primary focus is characterization. She notes that Vargas Llosa's novel can also be compared to Sartre's *The Reprieve*: "Indeed, as in *The Reprieve*, there are moments when the 'characters' are named but then dissolve back into the chorus of the text so that their discourse is identifiable only when new information becomes available to the reader."[17] Her comparison between *Conversation in The Cathedral* and *The Fall* is based on the parallel between the "confession" made by Clamance in a "church" — the Mexico City Bar in Amsterdam — and the "confession" that Santiago makes to Ambrosio in their "church," "The Cathedral" bar in Lima. This analysis leads to Franco's noteworthy observation about the conversation between Santiago and Ambrosio: "What takes place in *Conversation in The Cathedral* is not a true dialogue between the journalist Santiago and the ex-chauffeur Ambrosio, but rather separate recollections that take the form of dismembered dialogues with other people in the past."[18] Franco concludes that Vargas Llosa, like Sartre and Camus, focuses the reader's attention beyond the creation of individual characters. Paradoxically, each of the three writers emphasizes the role of the individual in society, yet each "create[s] literary projections of the individual that verge on impersonality."[19]

Mary Davis describes a reading of *Conversation in The Cathedral* by comparing it to Faulkner's *Sanctuary*.[20] Seen in the context of Faulkner, Vargas Llosa has created in Cayo Bermúdez a character parallel to Faulkner's Popeye. Davis observes that Vargas Llosa amplifies Faulkner's method of characterization: "Whereas Popeye's relationship with other characters is by means of objects, that of Cayo is by means of intermediary characters."[21] Vargas Llosa also creates an atmosphere similar to Faulkner's. *Conversation in The Cathedral* and *Light in August* have comparable plot development: Faulkner never clearly reveals that Joe Christmas killed Joanna Burden, and Vargas Llosa leaves the death of Hortensia ("the Muse") ambiguous.

Structure and Plot

In line with *The Time of the Hero* and *The Green House*, plot itself is an important factor in this novel. The stucture, however, marks a change: it is the author's first novel without a systematic division of narrative segments within all the chapters. He originally planned to publish the four-part book as four separate volumes. The first edition in Spanish consisted of two separate volumes, each containing two parts of the novel. Later editions in Spanish, and the English version, have been printed in one volume.

Each of the four parts is composed of between four and ten chapters. Part I (190 pages) consists of ten numbered chapters with no formal division within any of them. Part II (134 pages) has nine numbered chapters, each of which is formally divided into eight to twelve unnumbered narrative segments. These brief narrative segments range in length from one to three pages. Part III (133 pages) consists of four numbered chapters which, like Part I, have no formal divisions. Part IV (134 total pages) has eight numbered chapters which, like Part II, have unnumbered narrative segments. Each chapter has either three or four of these narrative segments, each ranging in length from three to seven pages.

Part I relates the early years of the Odría regime, begining approximately in 1948. Odría himself does not appear directly in Part I (nor anywhere else in the novel). The two main characters portrayed in Part I are Santiago Zavala and Cayo Bermúdez. Santiago is the son of Fermín Zavala, an affluent businessman belonging to Peru's powerful oligarchy. Cayo Bermúdez is the Director of Security for Odría's government. Part I encompasses Santiago's years as a student at the University of San Marcos and Don Cayo's rise from anonymity to a position of supreme power in the Peruvian government.

The novel actually begins in a "present" of the 1960s. The now thirty-two-year-old Santiago Zavala encounters Ambrosio Pardo, former chauffeur for Santiago's father, Fermín, and also for Cayo Bermúdez. Ambrosio is working at a dog pound where Santiago goes to claim his missing dog. The two spend four hours in intense dialogue at The Cathedral. Their dialogue, in turn, is transmuted into other dialogues and anecdotes, which in their totality relate the story of their respective lives and those of many other individuals during the time span from about 1948 to the early 1960s.

Santiago's story begins with his conflicts within his family. Unlike his brother, Sparky, and his sister, Teté, he is unwilling to accept the social values of his oligarchical family or the policies it supports. Against the wishes of his family, Santiago insists upon study at San Marcos, a university open to working-class students and, as viewed by the oligarchy, associated with leftist ideologies. Santiago becomes involved in politics with a group of student friends. He and Jacobo vie for the attention of Aída. Betrayed by Jacobo, Santiago loses Aída to him. Santiago continues his readings of Marxist ideology and, reviewing that period in retrospection, observes that "At that time I still envied people who

had a blind faith in something . . . "[22] At the end of
Part I, Santiago is arrested because of his political activities. He decides, then, to leave his family's home
and live independently — quitting school to work at the
newspaper *La Crónica*.

Cayo Bermúdez's story begins in the third chapter
(pages 39–58) of Part I. His ex-classmate, General Es-
pina, brings him from a town in the provinces, Chincha, to become Peruvian Director of Security in 1948.
Don Cayo's rise to power from his previous life as an
obscure local businessman in Chincha is spectacular
and horrifying. He soon becomes Odría's "other self," as
he is described in the text (p. 53). His basic method, as
recounted in the seventh chapter (pp. 111–33), is to
acquire power by overstepping and neutralizing everyone in the government except Odría himself. Don Cayo's
story blends directly with Santiago's for the first time at
the end of Part I. When Santiago is arrested for his
political activity, he is in the hands of Don Cayo.

Many other characters, some of whom will grow
in importance later in the novel, appear in Part I. Ambrosio is present as Don Cayo's chauffeur. A chapter
featuring Amalia and Trinidad (pages 75–89) provides
a working-class point of view on the political events of
the period. The reader observes Fermín not only as
Santiago's father but also as one of Don Cayo's collaborators from the business sector.

People, places and events that initially seem to be
unrelated appear in Part I. The reader does not find a
total clarification of all the details, but rather has the
aesthetic pleasure of participating in the unfolding of a
pattern. The reader's initial sign that this is a book of
patterns rather than incoherent fragmentation can be
found in the first chapter: early in it, Santiago mentions his newspaper campaign against rabies and later
in the same chapter he meets Ambrosio, who has found
employment at a dog pound precisely because of the
newspaper campaign. It is a coincidence that provides

the reader with an initial assurance that this is a novel in which events will eventually fit together. Nevertheless, Part I does project some unanswerable questions. Brief dialogues with Fermín speaking appear in the text inexplicably. For example, in the third chapter Fermín is quoted as follows:

— ¿Por mí, por mí? — dijo don Fermín — ¿O lo hiciste por tí, para tenerme en tus manos, pobre infeliz?[23]

"For me, for me?" Don Fermín asked. "Or did you do it for yourself, in order to have me in your hands, you poor devil?" (p. 57).

These questions on Fermín's part stand isolated in the text, with no context that might provide a clue as to what they refer to or with whom he is speaking. In addition to these rare pieces of dialogue by Fermín, there are equally mysterious one-sided dialogues articulated by Ambrosio in the seventh chapter (pages 111–33). The chapter begins:

— Estaba preso por haber robado o matado o porque le chantaron algo que hizo otro — dijo Ambrosio — .Ojalá se muera preso decía la negra. Pero lo soltaron y ahí lo conocí. Lo vi solo una vez en mi vida, don (p. 130).

"He was arrested for stealing or for killing somebody or because they grabbed him for something someone else did," Ambrosio said. "'I hope he dies in jail,' the black woman said. But they let him out and then I met him. I only saw him once in my life, sir" (p. 111).

The text that follows is a dialogue totally unrelated to Ambrosio's statement, and such one-sided dialogues by Ambrosio appear sporadically throughout the chapter. The sole pattern in Ambrosio's unidentified dialogue is internal: in each he speaks in a past tense ("dijo" in Spanish; "said" in English) and addresses his listener as "don" (translated "sir" in English).

These dialogues involving Fermín and Ambrosio will appear throughout the novel, but cannot be fully

understood until Part IV, when it is revealed that Ambrosio has, surreptitiously, been Fermín's homosexual
partner; the secret dialogues have been between them.
Similarly, there is an ongoing dialogue between Santiago and Carlos throughout the eighth chapter (pages
134–49) of Part I, for which the reader will have no
context until later in the novel.

Part II places more emphasis on Don Cayo and
Ambrosio. Don Cayo now has absolute power in the
Odría government. His men — Ambrosio, Ludovico,
Hipólito, and others — carry out his organized manipulation of the political scene: they organize political ral-
lies that give the appearance of mass support for Odría;
they repress and terrify government opposition parties;
they respond to all of Don Cayo's personal and political
whims. Don Cayo's private wishes are imbued with
sexual perversity. He takes voyeuristic pleasure in
watching lesbian activities. Ambrosio, too, appears in
the context of a love affair with his girlfriend and wife-
to-be, Amalia.

Santiago, now working at *La Crónica* and isolated
from his family, meets occasionally with his uncle
Clodomiro. His brother, Sparky, eventually contacts
him too. A strike that takes place at the end of Part II
appears to mark the end of Odría's regime. Don Cayo is
rumored to have escaped to Brazil.

Part III features the most frenetic activity of the
novel. The first chapter (pages 331–70) begins with
melodrama: Santiago and his colleagues at *La Crónica*
go to the scene of the Hortensia's (the Muse's) death to
investigate the story of her being knifed. Don Cayo's
loss of power develops concurrently with the downfall
of the house of prostitution he had supported in the
neighborhood of San Miguel. Chaos in both the narration and the story ensue in the last chapter, the fourth
(pages 432–64). Don Cayo sends Ludovico and a gang
of thugs to the city of Arequipa to interrupt an anti-

government rally there. A plethora of dialogues, some
by telephone, relate the story of the gang's sound defeat: some die and others barely escape alive. Don Cayo
and his government have lost in their final attempt to
control Peru.

Part IV further develops certain personal relationships and bestows upon the reader long-awaited revelations. Santiago scandalizes his parents by marrying
Ana, a girl of far too humble origins for the social
stature of the Zavala family. He also repudiates the
family one last time by refusing to discuss the inheritance after Fermín's death. Ambrosio marries Amalia
and they move to Pucallpa where he attempts, unsuc-
cessfully, to operate a business with a friend. Throughout Part IV there is an ongoing dialogue between Ambrosio and the prostitute whose services he uses, Queta.
It is in conversations with her that Fermín's homosexual relationship with Ambrosio is revealed. Fermín had
abused him sexually during visits to Ancón. The novel
ends, as it had begun, in the "present" of the dialogue
between Santiago and Ambrosio in The Cathedral.

Almost all the pieces of a narrative puzzle have
fallen together by the conclusion of the novel: the work
is very much a whole, with a sense of closure. One
critic, generally a sound reader of contemporary fiction, was so satisfied with this wholeness that he said:
" . . . we certainly get to know the truth about everything. The title, that is, is addressed to us, to the readers of the book; it is a signpost to the book's major
meanings."[24] Such statements are misleading and inaccurate, for even though the reader can understand how
the novel could lead one to such a conclusion, in reality
we get to know the "truth" about practically nothing.
The reader is offered many possible truths in the novel,
but most are merely relative; truth, like reality, is
amorphous and is only a matter of circumstance and
situation. As the circumstance and situation change, so

do an established sense of truth and reality. The reader
never apprehends the full truth, for example, behind
the death of Hortensia. At first, Queta leads the reader
to believe that Don Cayo had Hortensia killed. A journalist inquires at the beginning of Part III: "Is Cayo
Shithead Cayo Bermúdez? Are you sure he ordered her
killed? That bastard's living a long way off from Peru,
Queta" (p. 352). On the next page, Queta claims that
Hortensia was extorting money from Fermín, and Fermín had Ambrosio kill her. Queta explains: "Hortensia
was getting money out of him, was threatening him
with his wife, with telling the story about his chauffeur
all over town" (p. 353). Given what the reader knows,
it is quite likely that Ambrosio did indeed kill Hortensia
to protect Fermín. In the end, however, there is no
verifiable, absolute revelation about Hortensia's death.
It would also be a difficult proposition for the reader to
answer Santiago's irritatingly persistent question: "At
what precise moment had Peru fucked itself up?" This
has as its corollary question: "At what precise moment
did Santiago fuck himself up?" Other questions and
ambiguities remain concerning the characters' motives
and the nature of Peru.

The four-part structure of the novel develops the
personal stories of individuals such as Santiago, Don
Cayo, and Ambrosio chronologically, in a general
sense. Consequently, the reader can eventually place
together the key events in their lives. Even though the
plot moves forward with regularity, the quality and
intensity of the experience changes in each of the four
parts. Part I is dominated by dialogue. The reader becomes acquainted with the characters and gets to know
Peruvian reality primarily on the basis of what characters themselves *say*. There is a directness of experience
unmitigated by narrative filter: characters speak for
themselves. The controlling narrator's ordering and
juxtaposition of dialogues, of course, does determine
the nature of this directness. Part II is also rich in dia-

logue, but there is more presence and mediation by a controlling narrator in the series of short vignettelike segments than in Part I. Consequently, the controlling narrator in Part II provides the reader with a more concrete sense of time and place than before. Parts III and IV function as did I and II. Part III projects the most intense experience of the book, by its constant series of dialogues juxtaposed: in the fourth chapter (pages 432–64), dealing with the strike in Arequipa, are as many as *eighteen* simultaneous dialogues, making it the most complex of the entire novel.[25] Part IV, like Part II, consists of narrative segments with the presence of a mediating narrator who balances them between narrative and dialogue.

Metaphorically speaking, all of the anecdotes within the novel emanate from the original four-hour conversation between Santiago and Ambrosio in The Cathedral. This conversation leads to multiple associations and other dialogues in the past. Such a generalization can only be metaphorical and not literal, however, since much of what supposedly emanates from the Santiago–Ambrosio dialogue could never have been known by either of them. In technical terms, there are three sources of information, three authoritative narrators: Santiago, Ambrosio, and the omniscient narrator outside the story.

Oviedo has described this novel as a "pyramid of dialogues" which expand in concentric waves from the top of the pyramid, the Santiago–Ambrosio dialogue.[26] A further distinction could be made between two general types of dialogues: those in which the dialogue functions primarily within its own temporal context and those which primarily tell a story of past situations. The dialogues of the first type, dealing primarily with events contemporary with the persons speaking, are the novel's predominant type. They include dialogues such as those between Don Cayo and his political collaborators, and between Ambrosio and Amalia.

These dialogues tell the story of those speaking, and of their contemporaries; they do not tell of others in the past. The second type of dialogue, which tells the past history of persons not speaking, is less frequent. The three important dialogues of this type are those between Santiago and Ambrosio in The Cathedral, the one between Santiago and Carlos in a bar called the Negro-Negro, and that between Ambrosio and Queta in a brothel. These three conversations have several characteristics in common: each takes place in a bar or brothel setting; each appears with some regularity throughout more than one chapter of the text; each, in effect, places together key events to allow both the speakers involved and the reader to make sense of the past. The secret dialogue between Fermín and Ambrosio is special. As in the dialogues of the first type, it deals primarily with the immediate situation of the two speakers; as in the dialogues of the second type, it appears regularly (although sparsely) throughout the text. The Fermín–Ambrosio dialogue functions for the reader more like the dialogues of type two in that it reveals what is a past unknown to the reader.

The four main dialogues can be visualized as four apexes that are the structural framework within which the entire novel is narrated:

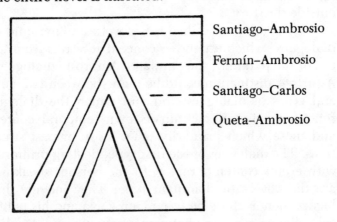

Santiago–Ambrosio

Fermín–Ambrosio

Santiago–Carlos

Queta–Ambrosio

These apexes, which relate to the past, provide the associative pretexts for the controlling narrator's direct moves into that territory.

Analysis of the story's anecdotal material suggests two general ways of reading this novel. By using Genette's concept of the nuclear verb, the novel could be conceived as an expansion of the sentence "A dictator corrupts Peru" (or, using the specificity and diction the text offers, "Odría fucks Peru").[27] Seen this way, Don Cayo's story is the visible arm of the dictator's acts of corruption. Peru's other problems and the problems of other characters are then an extension or result of Don Cayo's act of corrupting. A corollary to Peru's being corrupted is Santiago's losing his innocence. The thirty-year-old himself thinks of his past experience as one of losing his "purity." By the end of Part I, Don Cayo's corrupting and Santiago's losing innocence become directly related when Santiago is arrested.

Another appropriate way of conceiving a nuclear sentence and, consequently, of so reading the novel, is as follows: "Santiago talks about Peru." The first two sentences proposed emphasize content as meaning; this second proposition emphasizes technique. As Ronald Christ has suggested, "meaning" lies in this novel not so much in the nature of the materials as in the nature of their presentation.[28] Santiago's "talking about Peru" is, to begin with, the broadest outline for the novel's structure, as seen in the diagram. An expansion of this nuclear sentence leads to the other dialogues and the development of the entire story. The most outstanding feature of the novel, read this way, is the act of talking (the four major dialogues)—the presentation and structuring of reality—rather than the nature of reality itself. The dynamism of the book is to be found more in the various narrative procedures related to its dialogic structure—for example, its various enigmas—than in the thematic implications of such actions. While not

totally contradictory, the two basic types of nuclear
sentences suggested here, both reasonable approaches
to the novel, provide an idea of the two essential factors
of the plot and structure of *Conversation in The Cathedral*: both the plot and how it is presented are the outstanding features here.

Theme and Technique

The complex and amorphous reality of *Conversation in
The Cathedral* derives from a multiple set of narrative
procedures. In the end, the reader may conclude — as
one critic has — that the complexity here is a false complexity: nothing complex is happening, relatively simple events are being related as if they were part of a
jigsaw puzzle.[29] Before the reader will be able to reach
such a conclusion, however, it will be necessary to experience a complex set of situations and even master a
series of sophisticated narrative techniques.

The type of dialogue conformation pioneered in
The Time of the Hero and fully exploited in *The Green
House* is even more fully developed in *Conversation in
The Cathedral*. The telescoping of dialogues, such as in
the Fushía–Aquilino narrative segments of *The Green
House* (see Chapter 3), becomes one of the major challenges to understanding precisely and fully what happens in *Conversation in The Cathedral*. In *The Green
House* Vargas Llosa frequently intercalates two dialogues that belong to different temporal and spatial
spheres; at a maximum level of complication he creates
telescoped dialogues with as many as three different
conversations in juxtaposition. *Conversation in The
Cathedral* contains passages such as the following,
which deals with the Arequipa uprising in Part III,
Chapter 4:

(1) "I was blinded," Ludovico said. "And the worst thing was the strangling, brother. I began shooting wildly. I didn't realize they were grenades, I thought I'd been shot from behind."

(2) "Tear gas in a closed place, several dead, dozens wounded," Senator Landa said. "Could you ask for anything more, Fermín? Even though he's got nine lives, Bermúdez won't survive this one."

(3) "I ran out of bullets one-two-three," Ludovico said. "I couldn't open my eyes. I felt my head splitting and I fell into a deep sleep. There were so many on top of me, Ambrosio."

(4) "A few incidents, Don Cayo," the Prefect said. "It seems they broke up the rally, they did manage that. People are running out of the theater scared to death."

(5) "The assault guards have started into the theater," Molino said. "There was something inside. No, I still don't know if anyone's been killed, Don Cayo" (pp. 454–55).

In accordance with the technique of telescoped dialogues, these five quoted do not represent a logical step-by-step conversation. Ludovico's statement (1) is continued when he speaks again (3), but neither of his dialogues is in sequence with the others that appear in the same textual space. Senator Landa's statement (2) is also unrelated to these dialogues that surround it: he is speaking with Fermín, although Fermín himself never responds in this chapter. The next statement (4) is the Prefect's affirmation to Don Cayo, which will not be answered for another half page in the text (p. 455). The last statement quoted above (5) is Molina's conversation with Don Cayo. Don Cayo will respond to Molina after an interval of two-thirds of a page of textual space. The dialogue Don Cayo has with the Prefect is separate from Don Cayo's dialogue with Molina.

This fourth chapter of Part III is the most complex of the book (and of all of Vargas Llosa's fiction) in telescoped dialogues. Eighteen dialogues operate

simultaneously in this chapter: Ludovico–Ambrosio,
Landa–Fermín, Prefect–Don Cayo, Molina–Don
Cayo, Téllez–Ludovico, Téllez–Molina, Llerena–
Paredes, Alvarado–Llerena, Don Cayo–Llerena,
Arévalo–Llerena, Landa–Llerena, Don Cayo–Paredes,
Arbeláez–Lova, Arbeláez–Llerena, Lozano–Molina,
Alcíades–Don Cayo, Lozano–Ludovico, and Arévalo–
Téllez.[30] The makeup of the dialogues in this intense
chapter is revealing: even though the physical action
takes place in Arequipa, the character with the largest
number of the eighteen total dialogues is Llerena, who
has six. Don Cayo has five. Of the two principle com-
municators in the novel — Ambrosio and Santiago —
Ambrosio appears in only one dialogue, and Santiago is
totally absent from the chapter.

The dialogues in the novel penetrate reality by
means of their multiple temporal and spatial origins.
They are not Vargas Llosa's only technique for creating
an effect of penetrating reality. For example, Santiago's
conversation with Aída leads to the following passage:

. . . a lo mejor no querría juntarse más contigo, Zavalita: te
odio, papa. Nos hacíamos preguntas pero no nos las hacíamos, piensa. Piensa: nos estábamos haciendo amigos. ¿Habrá
estudiado en un Colegio Nacional? Sí, en una Unidad Esco-
lar, ¿y él? en el Santa María, ah en un colegio de niñitos bien
(p. 78).

. . . she probably wouldn't want to meet you anymore,
Zavalita: I hate you papa. We asked each other questions but
we didn't ask each other anything, he thinks. He thinks: we
were getting to be friends. Could she have studied at a national high school? Yes, in a central school, what about him?
at Santa María, ah, a school for rich boys . . . (p. 63).

A passage such as this does not intercalate dialogues
but, rather, thoughts with dialogues. The paragraph is
a combination of Santiago's interior monologue (i.e., "I

hate you, papa") and a dialogue between Aída ("Yes, in a central school") and Santiago ("at Santa María"). This type of paragraph, with few punctuation marks to indicate the transitions from interior to exterior communication, is one of Vargas Llosa's techniques for capturing the totality of the situation.

Vargas Llosa achieves several effects by his use of telescoped dialogues and similar techniques, such as the passage cited above. The intricate set of eighteen dialogues dealing with the Arequipa incident (Part III, Chapter 4) offers a simultaneous insider's and outsider's view of the events at hand. Characters like Ludovico and Ambrosio are the insiders, and are able to tell the Arequipa story as participants; the dialogues with Don Cayo, Fermín, and others communicate how the event was perceived from the outside — in addition to the role they had as distant participants from Lima. The juxtaposition of dialogues affords the reader the opportunity to observe and judge the contradictions and paradoxes of different situations. A humorous paradox occurs, for example, when the author juxtaposes a past conversation between Santiago's college peers, Jacobo and Aída, and the "present" conversation between Santiago and Ambrosio:

"Except for that of the proletariat, all dictatorships are the same," Jacobo said.

"Historically." [past]

"Do you know the difference between Aprismo and Communism?" Santiago asks. [present]

"We can't give him time to become the worst," Aída said. "We have to overthrow him before that." [past]

"Well, there are a lot of Apristas and only a few Communists," Ambrosio says, "What other difference is there?" [present] (p. 69).

The fact that Ambrosio, the "proletariat" who

would supposedly benefit from the revolution that
Jacobo, Aída, and Santiago discuss, cannot even distinguish between Aprismo and Communism, is not just
ironic but humorous. This type of paradox forces the
reader to construct a world vision similar to the one
that Santiago develops. It is a vision of reality that
eventually causes virtually any affirmation to be ne-
gated or contradicted. Santiago's vision of things develops this way both on the basis of his own experience of
1950s Peru and from what he learns in the conversation
with Ambrosio. In one interchange between the two,
for example, Santiago explains that he thought his father had fired Ambrosio, and Ambrosio responds as
follows: "What an idea, just the opposite. He asked me
to stay on with him and I refused. See how wrong
you've been son?" (p. 151).

The central dialogue, between Santiago and Ambrosio, is a special type of communication between the
upper-middle-class Santiago and the working-class
Ambrosio. For Santiago the conversation is an intellectual exercise with a psychological function; Ambrosio
tends to talk on a much more literal level. Their antagonistic discourse might be seen as an ideologeme — the
smallest intelligible unit of the essentially antagonistic
collective discourses of social classes.[31] Santiago, in attempting to explain to Ambrosio his obsession with
"purity" during his college years as an ideologue, creates the following interchange:

> "Revolutions, books, museums," Santiago says. "Do you
> see what it is to be pure?"
> "I thought that being pure was living without fucking,
> son," Ambrosio says (pp. 70–73).

There are numerous interchanges of this sort between
the two that suggest the difficulty of genuine communication between the social classes. Ambrosio does provide information and anecdotes that are quite revealing

to Santiago. The process of synthesis and arriving at a new self-awareness, however, is strictly that of the educated Santiago.

Narrative point of view in *Conversation in The Cathedral* is one effective vehicle for communication. If ideology is not seen as somehow "poured into" the text but as the very fabric of textual organization, an approach to Vargas Llosa's achievement can be made.[32] A key element to the text's organization is the use of an omniscient narrator who reveals the thoughts and feelings of characters at all levels of the social scale: Santiago, Ambrosio, Don Cayo, and even the humble Amalia. The narrator's distance from Santiago varies from chapter to chapter, but his discourse is often closely linked to Santiago's language or thoughts.[33] The eighth chapter of Part I begins:

La librería estaba en el interior de una casa de balcones, se cruzaba un trémulo portón y se la veía arrinconada allá al fondo, abarrotada y desierta. Santiago llegó antes de las nueve, recorrió los estantes del zaguán, hojeó los libros averiados por el tiempo, las revistas descoloridas. El viejo de boina y patillas grises lo mira con indiferencia, querido viejo Matías piensa, luego se puso a observarlo con el rabillo del ojo . . . (p. 155).

The bookstore was inside a building with balconies, you went in through a vague entranceway and from there you could see it huddled in back, barred and deserted. Santiago arrived before nine o'clock, scanned the bookcases in the entrance, thumbed through the time-worn books, the faded magazines. The old man with a beret and gray sideburns looked at him indifferently, good old Matías he thinks, then he began to look at him out of the corner of his eye . . . (p. 134).

An omniscient narrator outside the story[34] narrates the first two sentences. What the reader sees, however, is similar to what Santiago sees. The narrator uses the verb "to see" to describe the scene: the English "you

could see" could have been translated into the more
impersonal "one could see" ("*se le veía*"). In effect,
Santiago sees, as does the narrator and the reader. In
the second sentence the narrator describes the bookstore owner as "the old man with a beret and gray
sideburns." Here the narrator not only sees what Santiago sees, but also uses Santiago's familiar language:
the definite article "the" in the phrase "the old man"
presupposes an acquaintance with the man. The passage then moves to what Santiago thinks. Another example of this type of procedure takes place in the
fourth chapter of Part I. In that chapter Santiago waits
to take the entrance examination at the University of
San Marcos. As one critic has aptly noted, a "scanning
motion which shows through the superficially objective
description which follows mirrors Santiago's point of
view as the confusion of the scene and the anxiety of the
candidates are duly noted."[35] Once again, the narrator's
point of view is closely associated with Santiago.

As the brief analysis of the above passages has already suggested, the important issue with respect to
point of view in *Conversation in The Cathedral* is not
"Who speaks?" but "Who sees?" The speaker in this
novel is always either a character in dialogue (or brief
interior monologue) or the omniscient narrator; the
subtleties of the text, however, are related to who is
seeing. This "seer" in the text can be identified as a
"focaliser."[36] In the passage cited above, the speaker is
an omniscient narrator, but the focaliser is Santiago.

Don Cayo often appears in roles that alternate between being the object of focus and functioning as focaliser. He appears in this dual role, for example, in the
following passage of Part II, Chapter 9:

Llegó primero Hortensia, sin ruido: vio su silueta en el um-
bral, vacilando como una llama, y la vio tantear en la
penumbra y encender la lamparilla de pie. Surgió el cubreca-

ma negro en el espejo que tenía al frente, la cola encrespada
del dragón animó el espejo del tocador y oyó que Hortensia
comenzaba a decir algo y se le enredaba la voz. Menos mal,
menos mal. Venía hacia el haciendo equilibrio y su cara ex-
traviada en una expresión idiota se borro cuando entró a la
sombra del rincón donde estaba él (p. 360).

Hortensia got there first, noiselessly: he saw her silhouette on
the threshold, like flame, and he saw her feel around in the
dark and light the floor lamp. The black coverlet rose up in
the mirror opposite, the curly tail of the dragon gave life to
the mirror on the dressing table and he heard Hortensia start
to say something and her voice got tangled up. Better, better.
She was coming toward him trying to keep her balance and
with her face wild with an idiotic expression that was erased
when she entered the shadows of the corner where he was (p.
321).

The reader's attention is focused on Hortensia
from the first line as she is viewed by Don Cayo. The
verb "to see" (*ver* in Spanish) appears twice in the first
sentence as Don Cayo sees her silhouette. The image in
the next sentence, of a "black coverlet," appears
through the eyes of Cayo-focaliser as he sees the coverlet
in a mirror. The following sentence ("Better, better")
transcribes, literally, what Don Cayo thinks or articulates verbally — probably the latter. After this interrup-
tion of the scene, with his words, in the final sentence
of the passage a focaliser outside the story creates a
visual field that includes both Hortensia and Don Cayo
("toward him" and "where he was"). Don Cayo's role as
focaliser is particularly noteworthy and effective in the
novel because of his psychological makeup as voyeur:
his personality is revealed more by what the reader
observes him *see* (and, indeed, sees with him) than by
what Don Cayo says or does.

Vargas Llosa employs several principal focalisers
who function as such regularly throughout the novel.

In addition to Santiago and Don Cayo, others are Amalia and Ambrosio. Besides a focaliser outside the story — who provides a more distanced and external view than the focalisers-characters — the following characters are the principal focalisers in Part I:

Chapter	Principal Focaliser
Chapter 1	Santiago
Chapter 2	Santiago
Chapter 3	Don Cayo
Chapter 4	Santiago
Chapter 5	Amalia
Chapter 6	Santiago
Chapter 7	Don Cayo
Chapter 8	Santiago
Chapter 9	Trifulcio
Chapter 10	Santiago

The two expectional focalisers in Part I are the working-class characters Amalia and Trifulcio. The fact that Vargas Llosa privileges a proletariat vision of social reality in this way is an example of how ideology functions as a part of the narrative texture, rather than as some kind of isolated thematic content.

Amalia's most regular presence as focaliser is in Part II. The series of often-bizarre events that takes place in Hortensia's household — prostitution, lesbian sexual acts, and Don Cayo's voyeurism — is presented to the reader either directly (as Hortensia sees) or indirectly (as she explains having seen) through Amalia as focaliser. The very first narrative segment of Part II presents Amalia as focaliser, as do the fourth (pp. 195–196), seventh (pp. 198–199), and tenth (pp. 202–204) narrative segments. When Amalia first takes employment in Hortensia's home she is unaware of Hortensia's sexual proclivities and her relationships with Peru's oligarchy. Amalia, as well as the reader, gradually comes to an awareness of the personal lives of Hortensia, her girlfriends, and their male customers. This awareness is attained almost strictly by visual means: Amalia and the reader learn on the basis of what they see. One of her first shocking moments is a revelation of what Amalia-focaliser sees (Part II, Chapter 1):

Una mañana Amalia vio la cama vacía y oyó el agua del baño corriendo. . . . El vaho cubría, todo era tibio y Amalia se detuvo en la puerta, mirando con curiosidad, con inquietud, el cuerpo blanco bajo el agua. . . . En la atmósfera humosa, Amalia vio aparecer el busto impregnado de gotitas, los botones oscuros. No sabía dónde mirar, qué hacer, y la señora (con ojos regocijados comenzaba a tomar su jugo, a poner mantequilla en la tostada), de pronto la vio petrificada junto a la tina. ¿Qué hacía con la boca abierta? (p. 231).

One morning Amalia saw her bed empty and heard water running in the bathroom. . . . The room was full of steam, everything was warm and Amalia stopped in the doorway, looking with curiosity, with uncertainty at the white body under the water. . . . In the foggy atmosphere, Amalia saw her breasts appear, covered with small drops of water, the dark nipples. She didn't know what to do, and the mistress (with cheery eyes began to drink her juice, butter the toast) suddenly saw her standing petrified by the tub. What was she doing there with her mouth open? (p. 204).

Like virtually any passage of this length in the novel, the above selection manifests several changes in focaliser and speaker. Amalia functions as focaliser at the outset ("Amalia saw") and again in the passage when the reader sees Hortensia in a tub as Amalia sees her. Once Amalia becomes fully aware of the situation — *sees* Hortensia nude — she becomes embarrassed. The process of seeing the total picture in this particular scene, as in all segments in which Amalia is the focaliser, is a gradual one. This use of focaliser has several effects: it tends to present bodies as pieces of objects

rather than as human beings; it portrays Hortensia's
entire household as a puzzle that is pieced together in a
step-by-step process; and it provides a literal and metaphorical "innocent" eye on one aspect of the oligarchy's
life in Peru.

The use of Amalia and Don Cayo as the two principal character-focalisers in those narrative segments
that take place in Hortensia's home provides one of the
starkest of the multiple contrasts within the novel.
They represent opposite poles with respect to the act of
seeing: Don Cayo purports to see everything that takes
place in Peru (from the most public to the most intimate), whereas Amalia's innocent eye is among the
most limited of the novel. The fact that the reader
experiences the visual world of both in the same setting
makes the contrast between the powerful and powerless, the wealthy and the poor, readily evident.

The Peruvian society that the reader sees is devastating. The predominant image of the nation, already explored in *The Green House*, is that of Peru as
brothel. Don Cayo, the most powerful character in the
novel, uses his entertainment privilege in a type of
brothel, Hortensia's home. According to Santiago's vision of reality, Peru itself is a brothel, as he explains to
Ambrosio when reflecting in The Cathedral: "Because
you're closer to reality in a whorehouse than in a con-
vent, Ambrosio" (p. 143). In a country where virtually
everyone seems to be reduced to prostitution, Fermín
plays out the role of prostitute in his relationship with
Ambrosio: "Let me be what I am, he says, let me be a
whore, Ambrosio" (p. 567). One critic of the radical
novel in the United States has demonstrated that prostitution is a common motif in dehumanizing social systems: "Since an inhuman system produces inhuman results . . . what unified the group was not plot or
characters but a particular view of life—that the su-

perimposing of one human being's will, or the will of
any group of human beings upon any others, is the
Great Crime."[37]

A society that reduces human existence to such
levels of debasement can make individuals as different
as Santiago and Don Cayo surprisingly similar. Santiago's verbal self-reflection in The Cathedral leads him
to the following realization: "And my whole life a lie, I
don't believe in anything" (p. 101). He arrives at this
conclusion at the age of thirty, after losing what he
regularly calls his "purity." Don Cayo, more experienced in Peruvian life, is a cynic from the moment he
arrives in Lima. Major Paredes says to him: "At first I
thought you were posing as a cynic. Now I'm convinced
you really are. You don't believe in anything or any-
body, Cayo"(p. 242). When Don Cayo falls from power, he explains to Paredes: "I'm going to give you one
good piece of advice. Don't even trust your mother" (p.
460). By the end, the two principal forces of the novel,
with totally different backgrounds and aspirations, arrive at quite similar attitudes.

An overview of the lives of four principal characters demonstrates what Oviedo has called four models
of frustration.[38] The four frustrated characters are Santiago, Don Cayo, Ambrosio, and Fermín. Santiago is
unsatisfied with all his possible roles: as the son of an
affluent businessman, as revolutionary, as bohemian,
and, finally, as humble local journalist. Oviedo sees
him as a model of the typical Peruvian middle-class
nonconformist of the Odría period: "An honest but in-
sufficient breaking with the system, which doesn't become either heroic or to be rejected but a fall into
emptiness."[39] Don Cayo ascends from virtual anonymity
in his small town to a powerful position in Peru, only to
eventually have his quest for power frustrated. Fermín
fails both as father and entrepreneur. Ambrosio repre-

sents "degree zero" of the human possibilities that his
social class has in Peru.[40] His numerous jobs and failed
business ventures lead him to his final fate: working in
a dog pound.

Story, Dialogue, and Melodrama

The two predominant and most significant acts in *Conversation in The Cathedral* are speaking and seeing.
The act of speaking is announced in the title, and actually determines the structure of the novel. Franco
claims that "Vargas Llosa projects a self radically separated from any continuity with the past and only able
to acquire ethical status by the conscious reinvention of
the project."[41] In reality, the self projected in the characterization of Santiago Zavala acquires its ethical status and identity through the act of storytelling. By telling his story to Ambrosio, and reconstructing the entire
story with Ambrosio's collaboration, Santiago spends
four hours attempting to constitute a self from the incidents and persons that have touched his life as part of a
complex network. He attempts to create some order out
of the emptiness, contradictions, paradoxes, and chaos
that this period of his life has represented. His particular kind of speaking — the act of storytelling — is thus
essential and not merely a frivolous or insignificant exercise in talking.

The reader's role with respect to the multiple stories offered is identical to Santiago's: he or she must
make judgments in order to constitute the total story.
Just as Santiago leaves The Cathedral with many questions resolved, but yet still with some nagging doubts,
so does the reader. There are not definitive answers to
such questions as Who killed Queta? Vargas Llosa does
create a sense of closure to the act of storytelling at the
conclusion of the novel by returning to the original

setting of The Cathedral. This closure, however, is a formal device and not a solution to the problems and questions proposed in the work. In this sense, the much-discussed "fatalism" and "determinism" of this novel are not a totally accurate description or even appropriate generalization about the novel's experience: Santiago's life, as constituted by his own act of storytelling, at the age of thirty, is still in flux during the novel's "present." Even though the general situation is unquestionably dismal, he is still acting as part of a process — indeed, believing yet *another* totally different story of his life — rather than simply existing in a predetermined pattern. Although neither Santiago nor Don Cayo is likely to place faith or trust in the types of individuals or institutions that have caused them failure in the past, both seem at least capable of continuing some sort of dialogue, of retelling a story.

If the "speaking" of this novel is associated with what Ronald Christ has called the "nature of the materials," or content, the "seeing" can be associated with the "nature of the presentation of the materials," or form. Speaking is one predominant vehicle of communication because dialogues are abundant in the novel and serve an important storytelling function for certain characters — above all Santiago — and the reader. Seeing, on the other hand, is the reader's means for direct experience in the fictional world, frequently a direct experience simultaneous to that of the characters. Such is the case in the scene in which Amalia and the reader concurrently discover Hortensia nude in a bathtub. Acts that the reader sees are a part of a "real" or "true" experience (to the extent that any fiction can be considered real or true), as opposed to those that are told in dialogue, which first must be believed before they are "real" or "true." This act of seeing establishes the radical difference between Santiago's and the reader's experience.

Conversation in The Cathedral is the apogee of
the first period of Vargas Llosa's novelistic career. Like
The Time of the Hero and *The Green House*, it deals
with political and social realities — but on a larger scale
than the two previous works. It is not predominantly a
political novel, but a story of individual lives deeply
affected by a particular political and social circumstance.[42] The reader's main concerns in Part IV, in fact,
are not political events or characters, but the personal
dramas of Santiago and Ambrosio, particularly as they
relate to the persons around them: Fermín, Amalia,
Ana, and Queta. The first chapter of Part III is a melodramatic approach to the death of Hortensia. This
touch of melodrama is more fully developed in Part IV:
the potential history of a dictator proposed on the novel's first page ("At what precise moment had Peru
fucked itself up?") has become in the end a narrative
account of Santiago's marriage to the humble Ana,
Ambrosio's problems with life in Pucallpa, and the like.
All of this seems to be the stuff of light and popular
fiction rather than of one of the major works by one of
Latin America's most serious novelists. These more
mundane and popular aspects of Vargas Llosa's fictional repertoire flourish in the next two works, *Captain
Pantoja and the Special Service* and *Aunt Julia and the
Script Writer*.

5

The Discovery of Humor: *Captain Pantoja and the Special Service* (1973) and *Aunt Julia and the Script Writer* (1977)

Readers who had associated Vargas Llosa's writing strictly with such lengthy and demanding books as *The Green House* and *Conversation in The Cathedral* could well have been surprised, if not openly disappointed with these two novels of the 1970s. Vargas Llosa's audience had learned by 1969 that the mastery of complex patterns of dialogues and intricate structures — an active participation with the text — was a labor rewarded by an intense and special experience. One also recognized several familiar features in *Captain Pantoja and the Special Service* and *Aunt Julia and the Script Writer*, but discovered that these two light novels were shorter and, generally speaking, less demanding than those of the 1960s. Readers unable or unwilling to distinguish between seriousness and sobriety might be unsatisfied with these serious but unsober novels.

The melodramatic aspects of life initially explored in the second half of *Conversation in The Cathedral* are fully exploited in these two later novels, and even exaggerated to humorous proportions. The laughter comes in them usually from situations: *Captain Pantoja and the Special Service* is the author's raucous satire of one of his most consistent targets of criticism, the military; the comic of *Aunt Julia and the Script Writer* arises from a variety of sources, but above all from his use of melodramatic radio soap operas and self-parody. These two novels are Vargas Llosa's entertainments.

In restrospect, Vargas Llosa's "discovery" of humor was not without precedents. The melodramatic situations in *Conversation in The Cathedral*, such as Amalia's love life and Santiago Zavala's marriage, certainly would have brought a smile were it not for the dismal context within which they are played out. The incongruities that permeate all of Vargas Llosa's novels are even more prominent in the two novels of the 1970s and are the basis for much of their humor. The juxtaposition of the characters' blatantly contradictory statements, achieved by the telescoping of dialogues in the early novels, creates paradoxes with humorous potential. In *Conversation in The Cathedral* Santiago Zavala explains his college days to Ambrosio: "Revolutions, books, museums. Do you see what it is to be pure?" The uneducated Ambrosio responds: "I thought being pure was living without fucking, son."[1] Such an exchange reveals a writer with an eye for the incongruities that are the stuff of humor.

Captain Pantoja and the Special Service

When this novel appeared in Spanish in 1973, it was part of a general trend in Spanish-American fiction toward an accessibility that had not characterized many of the major novels of the 1960s.[2] The idea of a "total novel" had produced such landmark works as

García Márquez's *One Hundred Years of Solitude* (1967), Fuentes's *Change of Skin* (1968), Vargas Llosa's own *Conversation in The Cathedral*, and Donoso's *The Obscene Bird of the Night* (1970). Although accessibility was obviously not an important issue for many eminent Spanish-American novelists in the late 1960s, by the early 1970s a general reaction had set in against these hermetic tomes.

One example of this more accessible fiction was a series of fantasies that García Márquez published in 1972: *The Incredible and Sad Tale of Candid Eréndira and Her Heartless Grandmother*. The young Mexican novelist, Gustavo Sainz, whose previous books had been limited to a strictly intellectual reading public, published a humorous best-seller in 1974: *La princesa del Palacio de Hierro* (The princess of the Iron Palace). Gustavo Álvarez Gardeazábal, a young Colombian novelist whose previous fiction was political and historical in the sense that *Conversation in The Cathedral* was, brought out a best-selling novel of parodic humor in 1974: *El bazar de los idiotas* (The Idiots' Bazaar). It was within this general context, of a period during which a large contingent of self-assured and well-established authors began to write a more accessible fiction — frequently in the humorous vein of *Captain Pantoja and the Special Service* — that this novel appeared.

Plot and Structure

Set in Iquitos, the Peruvian Amazon jungle, this novel tells the story of the military officer par excellence, Captain Pantaleón Pantoja. His superiors send him to the jungle to solve a problem that has proved embarrassing for the government: the soldiers posted in these remote areas have been molesting the local females with alarming frequency and gravity. Pantoja, the quintessential military officer from the point of view of the army officers, receives orders to go to Iquitos as an undercover officer and organize regular sexual activity for the soldiers. His astonishing success at this enterprise, in addition to other local factors beyond his control, eventually causes his downfall. Both his methodical approach to the task and the bizarre anecdotes that accompany this central story—such as the presence of a fanatical religious cult—make the story often hilarious.

By utilizing Genette's concept of the nuclear verb to essentialize what happens in the story, it may be shown that the novel is an expansion of the basic sentence "Pantoja organizes prostitution for the military in Peru."[3] The verb "organizes" highlights Pantoja's methodical planning of the operation. The first chapter, written entirely in dialogue, introduces the "organizing" by showing Pantoja receiving his assignment and underlining his ability as an organizer. Others characterize him as an "innate organizer," with a "mathematical sense of order, executive capacity," and an "organizing brain." The midpoint and end chapters are exclusively dialogue, as is the first, whereas the remaining chapters portray Pantoja's "organizing" by means of military documents, messages, letters, newspaper articles, and conversations. These communications appear in addition to short passages related by the omniscient narrator. In the second chapter Pantoja himself describes the intimate details of his organization via official communiqués, all supported by data in scientific experiments. By the third chapter, Pantoja's mania for organization has reached such extremes that he relies on a stopwatch to calculate precisely his own sexual performance with his wife. Approximately halfway through the novel, Pantoja's failure is precipitated by his success as organizer, for his operation has acquired its own dynamics over which the military fears it has lost control.

A turning point in Pantoja's enterprise is a public denunciation by a local radio commentator named Sinchi. On his special program, *The Voice of Sinchi*, the radio hero asks rhetorically:

How long are we going to continue tolerating in our beloved city, my distinguished listeners, that shameful spectacle which is the existence of improperly named Special Service, more commonly known as Pantiland, in ridiculous homage to its founder? *The Voice of Sinchi* asks: How long, fathers and mothers of families in refined Loreto, are we going to continue suffering the anguish of shielding our innocent and inexperienced, our ignorant children from the danger they run in being exposed, as though it were some carnival or circus, to the traffic of courtesans, of shameless women — of *prostitutes*, to stop speaking of euphemisms — who brazenly come and go from that den of iniquity erected at the gates of our city by the unlawful and unprincipled individual answering to the name of Pantaleón Pantoja?[4]

Sinchi encourages one of Pantoja's ex-employees, a prostitute named Maclovia, to tell her story on the air. She, too, admires Pantoja's capacity as an organizer: "He's got everything so well organized — another craziness of his is order. All of us used to say this seems like a barracks, not a brothel" (p. 153). As expected, Pantoja's success as organizer causes his doom: he loses his position in the jungle and is assigned to a remote and undesirable provincial town.

The basic structure, or organization of the chapters within the novel, divides the ten chapters into four parts. The four parts develop four stages in Pantoja's organizing. (It is important to understand that the novel is formally divided into ten chapters; the four-part structure is my description of the organization.) The first part, which recounts the establishment of the operation, comprises Chapters 1 through 4. Part II, the

expansion of the operation, consists of Chapters 5
through 7. Part III, Chapters 8 and 9, relates Pantoja's
downfall. Chapter 10, the last, functions as a type of
epilogue.

The first chapter of Part I, containing dialogue on
various temporal levels, suggests much of the plot that
will be developed in the remainder of this early section.
The reader notes in the dialogue (the "present") between Pantoja and his wife, Pocha, that the protagonist
is obsessed with his military profession and that they
have started on a new assignment. In a dialogue revert-
ing to an earlier temporal plane, an unidentified
"past," the reader observes Pantoja receiving his assignment. Later the reader will become an active witness to
the outcome of the conversations interspersed in the
initial chapter. A mysterious voice appears near the
beginning of the chapter: "That's how it is, dear listeners," bellows Sinchi. "Neither fear of God nor respect
for His sacred house nor the noble hairs of that digni-
fied matron, who has already given two generations to
Loreto, were able to restrain those sacrilegious, those
lustful men" (p. 5).

This voice appears nowhere else in the chapter and
only later will be explained to the reader as that of a
popular radio announcer. Similarly, the voice of a religious fanatic, Brother Francisco, appears five times in
the first chapter and is ambiguous in the first part of
the novel. The second through fourth chapters describe
Pantoja's establishment from various perspectives: military communiqués written by Pantoja and other officers; a letter written by Pantoja's wife to a friend; a
narrative segment told by the omniscient narrator.

Part II marks the expansion of the operation. Like
Part I, it begins with a dialogue between Pantoja and
Pocha, which is soon intercalated with other dialogues,
making the chapter progressively more intricate. Two
important changes of Part II, which will be further de-

veloped, are suggested. First, in a dialogue between Pantoja and Pocha, his wife complains: "At first it bothered you to be a spy. You had nightmares and you cried and shouted in your sleep. But now I see you love the Intelligence Service" (p. 87). Also, in the intercalated dialogue among the military officers, it is already suggested that "the mistake was in starting. Now the avalanche can't be stopped. Each day the requests will continue to increase" (p. 94). The apprehension indicated in "Now the avalanche can't be stopped" is fulfilled when the operation later becomes problem-laden. Pantoja receives an initial threat in an anonymous letter, written by Sinchi but signed "XXX." Maclovia writes to Pocha to ask for her aid in returning to Pantoja's operation. The expansion noted in Part II is exemplified in these letters; they indicate that the expansion has meant an increasing *public* knowledge of the operation that culminates with Sinchi's denouncing Pantoja on his radio program (Chapter 7).

Part III, consisting of Chapters 8 and 9 and identified as the stage of Pantoja's downfall, presents various troubles. The dialogue chapter opens with a conversation between Pantoja and Leonor, his mother, substituting for the departed Pocha — for the operation has brought the end of his marriage. The intercalated conversations among the military officials hint at other problems. Sinchi's radio program, a public speech by Pantoja in honor of the deceased prostitute "the Brazilian," and a series of articles in the newspaper mark the public revelation of the venture, and Pantoja's demise.

Part IV, Chapter 10, is truly an epilogue because the organizing is now a *fait accompli*. It only remains to be seen what will be Pantoja's fortune. His life returns to the initial order and harmony of the first chapter. In the last paragraph Pocha has evidently returned to him in his new assignment in Pomata. Her comment

that he is a "maniac" in his work in Pomata discloses
that he is again obsessed with military order and discipline.

The novel's basic structure is a piece of precision
clockwork that recalls the dramatic structure of a traditional three-act play: Part I establishes the conflict,
Part II complicates it, and Part III resolves it. The dialogue chapters (1, 5, 8, and 10) serve as introduction to
each part, foreshadowing those changes in the development of the novel that the reader will actually experience directly in the course of the story. Three factors
create a sense of circularity and closure: (1) General
Scavino's prediction at the beginning of the novel is
fulfilled by Pantoja's failure; (2) Sinchi's brief presence
in the first chapter culminates in his key role at the
conclusion; and (3) the opening dialogue between Pantoja and Pocha is complemented by the reestablishment
of harmony when they return together, and sealed
when she repeats, as in the opening conversation,
"Wake up, Panta" (p. 244).

Theme and Technique

Several of Vargas Llosa's recurrent themes and preoccu-
pations (the military, for example) and oft-used techniques (such as telescoped dialogues) are present in
Captain Pantoja and the Special Service. But the complete change in tone and new narrative techniques of
this novel underscore his versatility. In addition to being an entertainment, it is, like the previous work, sub-
versively critical of the society it describes.

Vargas Llosa articulates social commentary by devices through which the incongruities in the process of
"organizing" are observed. He consistently juxtaposes
sexual proclivity with the military repression of such
impulses. The point of departure for such juxtaposition

occurs in the initial conversation between Pantoja and
his wife, Pocha, in the first paragraph of the novel:

> "Wake up, Panta!" Pochita is saying. "It's eight o'clock
> already. Panta, Pantita."
> "Eight already? God, I'm tired," yawns Pantita. "Did
> you sew on my new stripe?"
> "Yes, Lieutenant, sir." Pochita salutes. "Oh, excuse me,
> Captain, sir. Until I get used to it, honey, you're going to
> continue being my little lieutenant."

Even in playful conversation such as this, the initial confluence of the personal intimate life and the
military code appears. A basic incongruity of the novel
is thus established by juxtaposing the military "lieutenant," "Pochita salutes," and "Captain" on the one hand,
and "honey" on the other. A similar technique, and
effect, can be observed in the first communiqué sent by
Pantoja. His mathematical calculations of the length of
time involved in the sexual act and the number of
monthly sex acts necessary to enable the soldiers to per-
form their military functions at their best are a similar
humorous juxtaposition of the military and the intimate. Once the operation has become a quasi-official
part of the military superstructure, the effect of the
juxtaposition loses its humor.

Appropriately, Pocha observes at this point that
Pantoja now cherishes his assignment ("But now I see
you love the Intelligence Service" [p. 87]), and the military becomes aware of the immanent dynamism of this
operation. Henceforth the vitality and movement of
the story stem from the conflict between Pantoja and
his opponents, and from Pantoja's affair with "the Brazilian." The juxtaposition no longer offers the humorous potential that it did before the prostitution became
integrated into the military superstructure. Significantly, the commentator Sinchi relies on the juxtaposition
as the basis for his campaign against Pantoja: "Yes,

ladies and gentlemen, this is the hand-over-fist money-
making business of the Pharaonic Mr. Pantoja: to con-
vert the jungle garrisons and encampments, the fron-
tier bases and installations, into little Sodoms and
Gomorrahs, thanks to his flying and floating brothels"
(p. 146). Although similar to Pocha's original statement
in the sense that it juxtaposes the military and the intimate, the original humor of the contradiction now becomes rhetorical bombast that, in effect, is a criticism
of the juxtaposition itself.

These incongruities become apparent through the
emphasis placed on the values and mentality of the military. An important example of this emphasis is a statement by Pantoja at the beginning of the novel when,
upon receiving his orders to "organize" as a civilian, he
is told by General Scavino: "But always think as an
officer" (p. 14). His actions, and those of his colleagues,
should be understood precisely as such: the manifesta-
tion of a military mentality. Technically, the predominance of the military is communicated through the
novel's style, both in the use of official communiqués
and in the actual choice of vocabulary in the content of
the message. Besides Pantoja's obsession with orderli-
ness, his dependence upon and idealization of common
sense reflect his military way of thinking. Thus, he explains his actions with the use of proverbs: "That the
undersigned is conscious of the obligation to initiate the
Service . . . keeping in mind the truth and wisdom
concealed in sayings such as 'Haste makes waste' and
'The early bird catches the worm' " (p. 29). Similarly,
his explanation for the lack of lighting in the house is:
"All cats look gray in the dark" (p. 30). In accordance
with this strict military mentality, Pantoja apologizes
because a hymn invented by the prostitutes does not
include mention of the navy.

Another significant aspect of the values apparent
in the novel is its exaltation of *machismo*. The focal

point of the anecdote is the degrading and mechanized sexual practices that Pantoja institutionalizes. The point of departure for such mechanization is Pantoja's initial scientific investigation. The operation is conceived to provide for maximum "efficiency."

As for narrative technique, four basic models describe the narrative situations that are offered by the variety of materials in the novel. The first model is communication situations that involve direct dialogue which the implied reader experiences as an outsider distanced from the story. The second model has a written message directed to a specific reader within the story. The third is a communication situation of the traditional omnisicent narrator outside the story, who relates the events to an implied reader outside the story. The fourth model involves a narrator within the story who directs a message to a general public, or broad audience, within the story. Each of the narrative segments in the novel can be placed into one of these four categories, and the models offer the opportunity of analyzing the organization of Vargas Llosa's discourse in more detail.

Falling in the first model, communication situations involving dialogue, are Chapters 1, 5, 8, and 10. A controlling narrator provides occasional short phrases to indicate the speakers in the dialogue, and the reader observes the conversations as they occur. Thus, the stage directions by the narrator are all in the present tense. The actual content of these dialogue chapters becomes more complex than the description of the communication situation might strictly suggest, because the "present" in the chapters involves the juxtaposition of various conversations. In short, Vargas Llosa uses the technique of telescoping dialogues (see Chapters 2–4).

In the first chapter there are three basic groups of speakers. Initially, the reader notes the dialogue among

the members of Pantoja's family: Pantoja, Pocha, and
Leonor. The time and place of this dialogue changes
from Lima at the outset, to the initial days of the new
assignment, and finally to Pantoja's return home, inebri-
ated, at the end of the chapter. The second group is the
religious cult of Brother Francisco. A third shows Pantoja outside his immediate family—first, with military
authorities and, later, at the end of the first chapter, in a
bar gathering information for his new mission. This
chapter offers a distanced reader the opportunity to observe Pantaleón's actions. Chapter 1 is, for the most
part, a behaviorist study of him, both on an interper-
sonal basis within his family and as the professional military man. Because the entire chapter evolves in a continuous present, it has the effect of offering the reader the
opportunity to compare different intercalated dialogues.
Thus, the confluence of the personal and military is attained by narrative artifice. The continuous present suggests that Pantoja is not a character in different stages of
development, but one who will act differently in different situations.

In the second model, a written message is directed
to a specific reader within the story other than the implied reader of the novel. The narrative segments that
form this model include military messages and reports.
Also within this category are some nonmilitary communications, such as letters by Pocha and Maclovia. As
for the military documents, they give the reader insight
into the military mentality that pervades the novel. This
context reveals Pantoja's military persona. Vargas Llosa
employs this context to satirize military language. It is
the total context that makes such phrases as "the institution's good name" ironic in these passages. Humorous
and satirical effects are created when the detail surpasses
normal expectations. Thus, the reader may laugh at
Pantoja's observation that the room he is investigating
contains exactly 1,323 square meters. In summary, con-

text and language are vital to the experience of those
sections of the second model. After the first chapter, the
reader has access to a context beyond these messages that
are being written, and thus becomes organizer himself
when he integrates the military messages and letters into
the total novel.

The third model, which involves an omniscient
narrator outside of the story who relates the tale to an
implied reader outside the story, is found in only three
sections. They center on Pantoja during three different
evenings—two in August 1956 and one in 1958. This
model adds traits to Pantoja's characterization previously absent from the novel, and they provide the only psychological penetration of Pantoja in the work. We see his
feeling of horror and fear toward the world. He appears
terrified and helpless in each circumstance, even though
situations vary in each of the three chapters. These sections contrast with the military persona characterized in
the second model. Further, they offer the only dia-
chronic portrayal of Pantoja in the entire novel, evoking
key moments in his past that the reader may use to appreciate the current circumstance more fully. Here Pantoja remembers his fears during a military ceremony
when he was a cadet. Such past events appear as flashbacks that occur during the three evenings. These three
sections provide overall order and unity to the novel,
situate the reader, and add credibility (a human dimen-
sion) to the characterization of Pantoja.

The fourth model, in which a narrator within the
story directs a message to a general public within
the story, emerges in the sections involving Sinchi on
the radio and in the newspaper reports. The first section of
this type begins within Sinchi on the radio. His opening
comments of self-characterization—describing his interest in public welfare—are ironic for the reader of the
text (although not necessarily for the public to whom
the broadcast is directed) because the reader enjoys a

larger context in which to judge him. Sinchi denounces
Pantoja's operation in his "Commentary of the Day."
The speaker changes when Maclovia tells her story of
life as a military prostitute, a tale based on anecdotal
material already familiar to the reader from the military documents. Given the change in context, the story
loses its humorous effect and functions as part of Pantoja's drama. It now has a dramatic, and at times melodramatic, effect.

The newspaper articles of Chapter 9 have a similar audience, but the role of the reader of the text is
changed. The reader assumes the role of organizer once
more, coordinating the details revealed in the newspapers to formulate the total story in all its details. As in
Conversation in The Cathedral, Vargas Llosa employs
one of his most favored techniques: the surprise revelation of key details at the conclusion of the novel. The use
of this fourth model allows the reader to discover such
details as an active participant in the novel.

Although surely a less demanding reading experience than Vargas Llosa's previous novels, *Captain Pantoja and the Special Service* exemplifies the precise control
of narration that is a consistent mark of his work. Con-
sideration of Pantoja's organization (the content) and of
Vargas Llosa's organization (the structure) reveals a novel that is a parody of military organization in both form
and content. This correspondence between content and
form, theme and technique, results in an esthetic experience for the reader and implies a critical function of the
work with regard to Peruvian society.

Fanatic attitudes lend themselves to humor, and
Vargas Llosa adroitly exploits the comic potential of
obsessive characters in this novel. He has consistently
shown a certain fascination with fanatics, such as Father García of *The Green House* and Cayo Bermúdez
in *Conversation in The Cathedral*; but *Captain Pantoja and the Special Service* is the first novel that features

a humorous portrayal of a fanatic who is a major character. *Aunt Julia and the Script Writer* represents Vargas Llosa's continuing interest in humor and his fascination with obsessive personalities.

Aunt Julia and the Script Writer

The fanatic character in this novel is a writer, Pedro Camacho, one of the most unforgettable creations in Vargas Llosa's fiction. Camacho is the prolific author of soap operas that are broadcast on the radio — an author who takes himself more seriously than a Balzac or Sartre. The prinicipal source of entertainment for us is Camacho. The protagonist, however, is not this Balzacian fabricator of home entertainment but a young, aspiring writer quite similar to Mario Vargas Llosa. The protagonist, in fact, is modeled after his creator, and is even named "Marito."

Both Pedro Camacho and Marito emanate from Vargas Llosa's life. In the early 1950s Vargas Llosa was in charge of news bulletins for Radio Panamericana. He had contact with a Bolivian attached to a neighboring station, Radio Central, also owned by the backers of Radio Panamericana. The Bolivian was, according to Vargas Llosa, quite a colorful person and was responsible for all the scripts in the soap operas that highlighted Radio Central's programming.[5] This diligent "writer" was enormously popular in Lima. Vargas Llosa claims that he was both amused and fascinated by the Bolivian script writer: "He was a truly picturesque character who worked like the devil, who had an extraordinary sense of professional responsibility, and who was very absorbed by his role as a writer and performer."[6] During this very period Vargas Llosa was becoming involved with writing himself. He also fell in

love with an aunt much his senior and married her,
against his parents wishes. All of this—the self-styled
Peruvian Balzac and Vargas Llosa's tumultuous first
romance—provides ample anecdotal material for
melodrama. His semi-autobiographical recounting of
his relationship with his Aunt Julia caused her to publish her own book in response.[7] The novel's wildest
ancedotes, however, are the product of Vargas Llosa's
imagination.

Plot and Structure

Aunt Julia and the Script Writer is a novel of one love
story and numerous soap-opera melodramas of intrigue, passion, violence, and similar material. The
odd-numbered chapters tell the story of Marito: his
apprenticeship as a writer and growing romance with
his aunt. The even-numbered chapters are nine radio
soap operas that appear in the text as Pedro Camacho
has written them for broadcast.

Vargas Llosa explained his original plan for the
novel as follows:

I would narrate accurately some episodes of my own life,
covering several months: the time during which I worked for
Radio Panamericana, how I met my wife, how my marriage
was, and all that the whole thing meant in my personal
experience, etc. To alternate between these two stories was a
little like presenting the front and back of reality, an objective
part and a subjective part, a real face and a made-up one. I
tried to do this in the novel, to alternate a chapter totally or
almost totally imagined, with a chapter of personal history,
authentic, documented.[8]

This is a description of the basic structure of the novel,
even though, as Vargas Llosa has admitted, the final
version is quite different from what he had originally
planned.[9]

The odd-numbered chapters are narrated by a first-person narrator in retrospect. An adult tells his own story of late adolescence. At the beginning, Marito is studying law at the University of San Marcos, working at Radio Panamericana, and, above all, aspiring to be a writer. In the first chapter he (along with his family) meets the teasing Aunt Julia and the pompous script writer at the radio station, who succinctly introduces himself as "Pedro Camacho: a Bolivian and an artist: a friend."[10]

The initial chapters provide an introductory characterization of each. The indefatigable Camacho appears as a caricature of a writer whose superficial production never discourages his utter seriousness of purpose. Social events with the family lead to Marito's relationship with Julia: they celebrate an uncle's birthday by going out to drink and dance, and on the way home Marito kisses her for the first time. At this stage in Marito's development as a writer, his creation is conceived mostly in terms of models. He is always planning on writing "in the manner of" renowned authors (Somerset Maugham, Maupassant, and others). As the odd-numbered chapters are developed, Camacho's popularity grows in Lima, Marito experiments with different approaches to writing, and the secret love affair with Aunt Julia becomes more intense. Pedro Camacho loses control of his soap-opera factory, confusing characters among his numerous weekly productions. He eventually becomes insane and is scurried off to an asylum — only to reappear at the very end of the novel as a listless and even more eccentric old man. Marito's affair with Aunt Julia leads to their scandalous elopement to a small town.

The even-numbered chapters offer nine soap operas, written by Camacho, in which the most humorous element is their aesthetic failure. They are poorly written and usually in poor taste. The first of these stories

(Chapter 2) portrays a young woman, Elianita, who is to wed Red Antúnez. The evening they make nuptial vows, it becomes apparent that Elianita is four months' pregnant — by Red's brother, Richard. The melodrama ends as follows:

Would Red Antúnez desert his reckless, foolhardy spouse that very night? Might he have done so already? Or would he say nothing, and giving proof of what might be either exceptional nobility or exceptional stupidity, stay with that deceitful girl whom he had so persistently pursued? Would there be a great public scandal, or would a chaste veil of dissimulation and pride trampled underfoot forever hide this tragedy for San Isidro? (p. 39).

All of Camacho's soap operas tell such a story and end with similar melodramatic interrogations. They often feature characters with sexual or psychological aberrations, who range from rapists to psychopathic murderers.

The structure of alternating chapters gives a special ending to the novel. By Chapters 17 and 19, Marito's situation has become critical. Chapter 20, which the reader expects to be another of Camacho's soap operas, is the final chapter of the affair Marito has had with his lover, Aunt Julia, and with his love, writing. In this manner Vargas Llosa implies that Marito's story has become another soap opera. Marito as narrator actually suggests such an idea: " . . . and Aunt Julia laughed when I told her that at one moment in my dreams I'd found myself living through one of Pedro Camacho's recent catastrophes" (p. 313). Despite the numerous suggestions of this sort, fundamental differences remain between Marito's story and those of Camacho. Differences in the discourse, content, and ending of the two make it inaccurate to conclude that by Chapter 20 the two story lines have in reality been synthesized.

Theme and Technique:
A Novel of Readers and Writers

Aunt Julia and the Script Writer presents four persons who are writers. The first, Pedro Camacho, appears in the chapters narrated by Marito.[11] Camacho can be described more precisely as a "scribbler," to use the term of Roland Barthes.[12] The second writer is Marito, the young narrator of the odd-numbered chapters. The third writer present in the novel can be identified as Pedro Camacho–narrator, who appears implicitly as such in the even-numbered chapters (text of the nine soap operas). It is important to make the fundamental distinction between an author (in this case the *person* Pedro Camacho) and a narrator (the fictional entity present in any narrative). The fourth writer is Mario Vargas Llosa himself, the author of several novels and, a notable factor here, of numerous critical and theoretical texts (see Chapter 7). Although never identified directly, Mario Vargas Llosa is recognizable by his name, of course, as the writer, and by the intertextuality, which will be discussed later. These four writers are related, and their potential relationships can be schematized as follows:

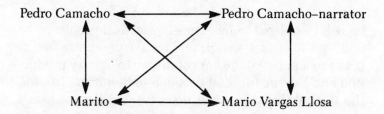

Each of the four writers potentially corresponds to the other three; the relationships suggested by these lines are the basis for the dynamic interaction among the "writers" of the novel.

Using the odd-numbered chapters as a point of departure, the reader realizes the relationship established between Pedro Camacho and Marito. Given the limitations of a first-person narration (Marito's narrative), the reader becomes acquainted with Pedro Camacho only according to what Marito is capable of observing and describing. The protagonist's information, like the reader's, is limited to encounters at the radio and a few other visits. Camacho's humorous self-characterization has a parallel thematic development in Marito's desire to be a writer. As the relationship between the two characters develops, the young writer learns of Camacho's daily life and his ideas about the art of writing. Marito tends to view all this as a matter of personal and artistic *style*. Inasmuch as writing is above all a matter of "style," his first stories are imitations of writers such as Borges, Twain, and Shaw. He is captivated by Camacho's discipline and total devotion to his chosen profession. Both the novice and the professional writer aspire to create art, even though the script writer is merely a compulsive scribbler without the capacity to grow intellectually or artistically. But Marito sees the attraction Camacho's creations have on Lima's radio listeners.

In addition to the issue of style, the relationship between Marito and Pedro Camacho reveals to the former that, in order to make himself a professional writer, he will be obliged to face certain practical problems: he will have to attract readers and resolve the contradiction between a personal life not conducive to literary production and a desire for total devotion to literature. In sum, the vertical line that unites these two entities suggests a problematic relationship of artistic creation that places before the reader this question: How does one resolve the essential conflict between the artist and professional?

With respect to the horizontal line in the paradigm between Marito and Mario Vargas Llosa, it should be clarified that they represent different persons. The former is a fictional character who can be considered *somewhat* similar to the young Mario Vargas Llosa. The author himself has affirmed that this character is a variant from the supposed autobiographical model.[13] A retrospective observation can be noted from the first line of the novel: "I was very young and lived with my grandparents in a villa with white walls in the Calle Ocharán, in Miraflores." A dichotomy is thus established between a "narrating-self" and an "experiencing-self."[14] The narrating-self is the adult writer, Mario Vargas Llosa, while the experiencing-self is the young Marito. There are several elements of tension between these two entities. Marito's useless attempts at imitating Borges and Hemingway are interesting for the contrast between the products of the narrating-self and the desires of experiencing-self; Mario Vargas Llosa differs from these writers.

The distance between the narrating-self and the experiencing-self logically diminishes as the novel progresses; at midpoint, the protagonist feels socially alienated as a consequence of his relationship with Aunt Julia and literature. Marito's writing begins to resemble his creator's texts by the end of the novel. Abandoning the imitation of other styles, he writes a "social story" closer to Vargas Llosa's constant concern about Peruvian society. Even more salient is Marito's conclusion that "everyone, without exception, could be turned into a subject for a short story" (p. 244) — a key point in Vargas Llosa's aesthetic theories. Marito writes an anticlerical story, "The Blessed One and Father Nicolas," both as a result of his frustration over the difficulties in marrying Aunt Julia and as an act of revenge. Therein lies another parallel with Vargas Llosa's fundamental ideas: the writer creates in order to gain revenge on the past or to liberate himself from cultural or social "demons."[15]

The last chapter, a type of epilogue, is a synthesis of the narrating-self and the experiencing-self and, conse-

quently, resolves the interaction between Marito and
Mario Vargas Llosa. In the hiatus of eight years between
the last chapter and the previous one, the amateur writer has become a professional: "I had become a writer
and published several books" (p. 358), he claims. The
reader outside the texts perceives the relationships between the author and the character, using information
known about the novels and essays of Mario Vargas Llosa
and even of his biography.[16]

The relationship between Pedro Camacho and Mario Vargas Llosa represented by the diagonal line joining
them in the above scheme opens the reader's eyes to
parody, humor, and intrigue. To fully appreciate this
line, a brief digression on the author's theories is helpful.
According to Vargas Llosa, the writer is a dissident who
practices the art of writing as an exorcism to liberate
himself from the "demons" encountered in society. The
novelist's role in society makes the act of writing a "nega-
tive participation" in life. Vargas Llosa always maintains
a humble attitude toward creation, identifying himself
as a "peon of novelizing"; this "peon" attains success by
virtue of his discipline and diligence, rejecting concepts
such as "genius" or "inspiration." Parallel to Vargas Llosa's insistence on discipline is his concept of the rigorous
reader. Describing his first encounter with *Madame
Bovary*, Vargas Llosa has explained how he read it obses-
sively: "As the afternoon went by, night fell and the sun-
rise appeared, the magical transformation was more ef-
ficient, the substitution of the real world by the fictitious
one."[17]

The relationship between Pedro Camacho and Mario Vargas Llosa is based on self-parody by the author,
the extratextual writer. Even though Pedro Camacho is
the fool, the scribbler ridiculed throughout the novel,
the pseudo-artist totally dedicated to his work, at the
same time he is a mirror image of his creator: Pedro
Camacho is amazingly similar to Mario Vargas Llosa.

Both are literature fanatics.Vargas Llosa praises discipline; Camacho practices it conscientiously in his soap
operas. Camacho explains: "I begin to write at first
light. By noon, my brain is a blazing torch. Then the fire
dies down a little, and around about dusk I stop, inasmuch as only embers remain. But it doesn't matter, since
the actor produces more in the afternoon and at night. I
have my system all carefully plotted out" (p. 41).

Later in the novel, Marito demonstrates a certain
admiration for literary obsessions. He states: "Three
things about Pedro Camacho fascinated me: what he
said; the austerity of his life, entirely devoted to an obsession; and his capacity for work" (p. 127). Despite the
characterization of the script writer as a fool, in this
context his similarities with Vargas Llosa are so notable
that one level of reading establishes parallels between
the two. The interaction creates a parody of Vargas Llosa's extratextual writings; i.e., works other than *Aunt
Julia and the Script Writer.*

The horizontal line between Pedro Camacho and
Pedro Camacho–narrator in our diagram suggests another type of relationship. Pedro Camacho appears as a
character in Marito's story; Pedro Camacho–narrator is
the implied author of the soap operas. Some aspects of
the humor in the soap operas are determined by the
interaction between these two entities. Camacho's inex-
plicable but vociferous prejudice against Argentines, for
example, becomes humorous in the soap-opera sections,
given what the reader knows about the narrator. An
acquaintance with Camacho as a person adds dimen-
sions to the soap operas. Despite the suggestions from the
radio personnel that listeners prefer young protagonists,
Camacho stubbornly presents them as older individuals,
thus creating humorous situations — describing one, for
example, "in the prime of life, his fifties." The relationship between Camacho-author and Camacho-narrator
is one of the principal elements in the dynamism of the

plot; it is evident that the character is becoming insane, confusing characters and mixing characters from different soap operas in an alarming fashion.[18] The reader judges Camacho's sanity on the basis of what he reads in the soap operas.

The vertical line between Camacho–narrator and Mario Vargas Llosa suggests a fifth level of interaction among the writers. Once again the dichotomy between the two types of chapters invites comparison, and in this case between the narrative technique in the soap operas and those in Vargas Llosa's other novels. Camacho–narrator's exaggerated, polished style, notable for its excessive number of adjectives, contrasts with the precise and direct language that characterizes Vargas Llosa's other writing, and with the chapters that deal with Marito. Camacho–narrator's excesses are apparent from the very first sentence of his first soap opera:

On one of those sunny spring mornings in Lima when the geraniums are an even brighter red, the roses more fragrant, and the bougainvillaeas curlier as they awaken, a famous physician of the city, Dr. Alberto de Quinteros — broad forehead, aquiline nose, penetrating gaze, the very soul of rectitude and goodness — opened his eyes in his vast mansion in San Isidro and stretched his limbs (p. 18).

This sentence features not only a simple and overused language, but also creates its own clichés by repetition. In the second soap opera, Sergeant Lituma is described, too, as having a "broad forehead, aquiline nose, penetrating gaze, the very soul of rectitude and goodness" (p. 60). In the soap opera that follows, Camacho-narrator uses the same formula.[19]

As far as point of view is concerned, Vargas Llosa has always been a faithful follower of the "objectivity" proposed by Flaubert.[20] And he has put the theory into practice: in his novels the omniscient narrator always maintains a position of neutrality as opposed to an editorial omniscience in which the narrator offers opinions. Consequently, when the soap-opera narrator interrupts his story to explain that the fifties are the "prime of life," such an editorial comment contrasts markedly with Vargas Llosa's theories and his previous novels. Camacho-narrator also tends to explain his characters through introductory portraits rather than revealing them through action and speech, as in Vargas Llosa's novels.

The sixth relationship in the paradigm, between Marito and Camacho-narrator, is the least important. Marito has direct contact with Camacho but, unlike the reader, he has no access to the nine soap operas intercalated in the text. Marito's awareness of Camacho–narrator, as has been noted, comes from his observing Camacho–narrator's enormous prestige among his listeners. This popularity affects Marito's writing and professional attitudes.

As the six lines of the diagram suggest, *Aunt Julia and the Script Writer* is a novel that deals with the relationship, manifest on various levels, of the writers fictionalized in the novel. Marito learns about the art of writing; one of the themes of the novel is this art, and the relationships among the writers gives the reader a prolonged experience of the act of writing itself. In this experience the reader contributes to the creative process, incorporating "theoretical" writings; and it becomes evident that the novel proposes a corollary to the problem of writing: reading. The reader is invited to resolve technical problems of readings, and the reader concurrently encounters the act of reading as a theme in itself.

Marito's career as a writer deals directly with a complementary problem: the reader. The young novelist discovers that his first obstacle to the attainment of literary success depends less on literary merit than on the reaction of his readers. He employs Aunt Julia as a reader, for example, and discovers for the first time the discrepancy between the author's perception of his literary creation and that of the reader. When he reads her "The Humiliation of the Cross," he notes that precisely what she criticizes are the imaginative elements. This anecdote is important for two reasons: first, as an example of Walter Ong's proposition that reading is an apprenticeship of conventions, a knowledge of things that she (Julia) still lacks;[21] second, as an early lesson in the realization that in the communication of fiction a new entity exists: the reader. In Wayne Booth's terms, it could be stated that Marito has not yet successfully fictionalized a role that his mock reader is willing to accept. Consequently, maturation consists not only in learning to write stories, but also in knowing how to invent a reader.

The reader of *Aunt Julia and the Script Writer* inevitably confronts a series of problems specific to the very act in which he or she is engaged. In this particular case the reader is presented with two types of chapters and can, logically, question what the function of simple soap operas is in a contemporary novel — especially when such creations make up half of the novel. The question can be set forth as follows: How can the reader of contemporary fiction (a supposedly sophisticated reader) deal with a novel half of which is composed of mediocre soap operas? They do serve as example of the activity of one of the main characters, but as an example one chapter would have sufficed. But the reader confronts a *series* of soap operas.

This problem can be considered by examining the the "mock reader" created for the soap-opera chapters. This fictional reader of the even-numbered chapters does not have the self-respect of the Mario Vargas Llosa reader of the previous novels, nor, to make a comparison with another writer, does this reader have the self-respect of the fictional reader of Hemingway.[22] If the subtle use of narrative techniques in the previous novels of Vargas Llosa (and Hemingway) functioned as a form of flattering the reader, here the reader is degraded, Vargas Llosa explains the most simple matters — which places us in a position of inferiority. This fictional reader is interested in crude violence and sex, and the mode of presenting these elements is melodramatic; this fictional reader enjoys a simple humor, such as, for example, a scene in which the secretary of a judge is fascinated by a promiscuous adolescent.

The "soap-opera reader" is seen disdainfully by the reader of the autobiographical chapters (the "Vargas Llosa reader"). The essence of the Vargas Llosa reader's experience is based on *observing the fictional reader of the soap operas.* Distanced from the violence, melodrama and simple humor, the Vargas Llosa reader is entertained by the fictional reader of the soap operas. The creation of this fictional entity — which contributes a level of understanding beyond a literal reading of the melodramas — is one of the principal achievements of *Aunt Julia and the Script Writer*. The fictionalization of this particular reader marks a culmination in the novels of Vargas Llosa in which the author exorcises, within the text, one of the "demons" he has discussed extratextually: the typical Peruvian reader.[23]

Aunt Julia and the Script Writer begins with an epigraph from a novel by the Mexican novelist Salvador Elizondo: "I write. I write that I am writing. Mentally I see myself writing that I am writing and I can also see myself seeing that I am writing." (Elizondo's solipsistic observations continue for several more lines.) Such commentary reflects a common attitude of writers during the 1970s, both in Latin America and elsewhere. *Aunt Julia and the Script Writer* can be seen as part of a general trend toward self-conscious fiction or, to use a term that the American writer John Barth has popularized, a literature of exhaustion. This is Vargas Llosa's novel about writing. Nevertheless, it has features that distinguish it from much metafiction. The dynamics of reading and writing (discussed in this chapter) make this novel more entertaining than much self-conscious fiction, which is often characterized as dry "writers' writing."

The novel is, in effect, ten stories: nine soap operas plus Marito's story. The interest in storytelling is consistent with Vargas Llosa's previous work and sets it apart from much of the "writing about writing" published in Latin American and elsewhere during the 1970s.[24] Vargas Llosa's humorous inventions of the decade set the stage for a movement toward a more traditional writing in his later work.

6

Synthesis: *The War of the End of the World* (1981)

Its epic vision, apotheosis of storytelling, and fascinating characters are just three of several factors that make *The War of the End of the World* a synthesis of Vargas Llosa's writing career. It is a vast (some 568 pages) and challenging novel set in rural northeast Brazil near the end of the nineteenth century. Vargas Llosa retells the incredible story of an anti-government rebellion by a community of religious fanatics and the ensuing war between these fanatics and the equally fervent government soldiers. As is all too often the case with such "incredible" Latin American stories, the happenings in the Brazilian town of Canudos are based on actual historical events during the late 1890s. This setting and historical context provide the anecdotal material for what is quite likely Vargas Llosa's best novel. Many of his previous attitudes, themes, and narrative techniques are fully elaborated in *The War of the End of the World*. Nevertheless, it is a more accessible novel than his previous work of epic proportions, *Conversation in The Cathedral*.

According to Vargas Llosa, he had "never been so fascinated with a story" as the one of Canudos.[1] His fabrication of it in novelistic form is the result of both chance and a labor of extensive research. Chance came into play when a Brazilian film director asked Vargas Llosa to write a filmscript for a movie using Canudos as

121

a sort of backdrop. Since the Peruvian knew nothing of
the subject, he read a classic book in Brazilian literature, *Rebellion in the Backlands* (*Os Sertões*, 1902) by
Euclides Da Cunha. Vargas Llosa then spent several
months writing the script — but the picture was never
made. Nevertheless, he decided to write the novel "because in the history of the Canudos war you could really see something that has been happening in Latin-
American history over the 19th and 20th centuries — the
total lack of communication between two sections of a
society which kill each other fighting *ghosts*, no? Fighting fictional enemies who are invented out of a fanaticism, out of religious or political or economic blind-
ness!"[2] The writing of this story was a four-year project
that involved a considerable amount of research (carried out at the Library of Congress). After writing a
draft of the novel, Vargas Llosa then went to Canudos
and spoke with inhabitants there and in neighboring
villages. "Everybody has a great uncle who was there, a
relative who died there," Vargas Llosa explains.[3]

The initial response among critics and readers to
this "adventure story," as the author himself has called
it, was uniformly enthusiastic. One of Latin America's
most respected and able critics, the late Ángel Rama,
judged *La guerra del fin del mundo* a masterpiece that
future generations would consider a key Latin American novel of the second half of the century.[4] It became
an immediate best-seller in the Hispanic world, and
remained so for over a year. The French translation was
a best-seller in France. When it appeared in English,
two years after *Aunt Julia and the Script Writer* had
popularized Vargas Llosa's name among North American readers, a reviewer for the *New York Times* called
it a "powerful and haunting" novel, and the *New York
Times Book Review* singled it out as one of the twelve
best books of the year.[5] Another review of *The War of
the End of the World* proclaimed Vargas Llosa one of

the "world's best writers."[6] Although accurate and truly balanced evaluation of any new book is often difficult, general consensus has been that this was one of the most outstanding novels by one of Latin America's most talented writers.

The Anecdotal Material:
Rebellion in the Backlands

Vargas Llosa has long maintained that the novelist and historian are closely allied: "Rescuer and verbal grave-digger of an epoch, the great novelist is a kind of vulture: the putrid flesh of history is his favorite nourishment and has served to inspire him to his most audacious undertakings."[7] In this case, Vargas Llosa the "verbal gravedigger" used an unusual text to unravel that "putrid flesh of history," for Da Cunha's *Rebellion in the Backlands* is an unorthodox combination of imaginative fiction, documentary history, and sundry essays. Da Cunha, after having worked several years as a journalist, was sent to Canudos in 1896 to cover the uprising for a newspaper known as *Estado de São Paulo*. Five years after the fall of Canudos, Da Cunha's magnum opus of more than 500 pages appeared, in 1902. Considered by some critics as Brazil's greatest book, and by many Brazilians as the "Bible of Brazilian nationality," *Rebellion in the Backlands* was an immediate popular success there.

To place Canudos in a general historical context: Brazil's people gained independence in 1899 when Dom Pedro II and the Empire were overthrown. The ruling aristocracy had already been challenged in 1888, when slavery was legally abolished. Forging a unified Brazil was a vital problem of the following period. Regional, political, and economic conflicts undermined stability, and, before Canudos, there had already been a counterrevolutionary revolt in 1893–94 that had threatened the nascent Republic.

The general setting of Vargas Llosa's novel was, therefore, rural northeastern Brazil, the town of Canudos and surrounding villages, and the city of Bahia. The Spanish edition of the novel featured a full-page reproduction of a painting of Canudos: the simple portrait shows an idyllic village with three large buildings (one of which is a church), a small cemetery (with twelve crosses), and a hundred or so little huts. Da Cunha had offered the following description: "Canudos, an old cattle ranch on the banks of the Vasa-Barris [river], was in 1890 a backwoods hamlet of around five-hundred mud-thatched wooden shanties."[8]

Background to the conflict was the arrival in Canudos in 1893 of a bizarre individual named Antônio Conselheiro; his life and personality were in themselves material for a novel. He had spent many years wandering through the backlands regions as a type of roving missionary — giving sermons and advice to the poor, living parsimoniously, and helping to repair local churches and cemeteries. In the process, he became a popular legend in his own lifetime; indeed, a Christlike figure. Da Cunha states that Conselheiro "looked upon the Republic with an evil eye and consistently preached rebellion against the new laws."[9] Once he settled in Canudos, his following grew rapidly, the town's expanded population was a motley crowd of the poor and outcast, including some of the region's most feared criminals. All were or became fanatic religious followers of Antônio Conselheiro. (In the translation into English of *The War of the End of the World* the narrator calls him "Antonio the Counselor," although some characters refer to him as "Antônio Conselheiro.")

His followers, the *jagunços* of Canudos, were soon faced with defending Canudos against four major at-

tacks by government soldiers. The fervent peasants
soundly defeated the government's first contingent of
one hundred. After the *jagunços* viciously destroyed the
second army of five hundred, the war in Canudos became an event of national significance. Consequently, a
renowned and successful colonel, Antônio Moreira César, with some twelve hundred soldiers, was sent to
Canudos. The confident Moreira César, and many of
his soldiers, were brutally massacred. An extended final battle with over three-thousand national troops,
supported by heavy artillery, razed Canudos and killed
its thousands of inhabitants.

Da Cunha's version of these incredible events is a
ten-chapter book that cannot be classified as either a
novel or historical analysis. The initial chapters consist
of the author's painstakingly detailed descriptions of
the land and people of northeastern Brazil — certainly
not exciting reading for the non-specialist not particularly concerned with the geographical contours of the
region — or his essays, such as the seven-page "Hy-
potheses Concerning the Origin of the Droughts."

Chapter 1, "The Land," is a combination of scientific data and impressionistic observations on the geog-
raphy of the area. It also includes such potentially
novelistic devices as offering a view "From the Top of
Monte Santo" and "From the Top of Favella." In Chapter II, "Man," Da Cunha affords the reader a bit of
historical, ethnographic, and sociological study. After
providing background to the origins of the *jagunços*
and essays such as "Reflections on Environment in History,"
the author moves from a description of the people to a
specific characterization of Antônio Conselheiro: "And
so there appeared in Bahia the somber anchorite with
hair down to his shoulders, a long tangled beard, an
emaciated face, and a piercing eye, a monstrous being
clad in a blue canvas garment and leaning on the classic staff which is used to stay the pilgrim's tottering

steps."[10] This chapter relates Conselheiro's life in considerable detail, including his image as a popular legend: "The popular imagination, as may be seen, was
beginning to make a romance of his life, displaying in
the process a tragic power of fantasy and a high degree
of originality."[11]

Chapters III through IX are the story of the conflict: a detailed account of the four major battles, and
related skirmishes. Da Cunha records the events with
precise detail: "It was here that 543 regular army men
were quartered, with 14 field officers and 3 surgeons —
the whole of the first regular expeditionary force in
Canudos."[12] In addition to the four lengthy battles, the
author describes individuals on each side, such as the
jagunço João Grande and Colonel Moreira César of the
government. Da Cunha always locates himself on the
side of the government: the soldiers are "our troops."
Nevertheless, during the seemingly endless final siege of
Canudos, the courageous *jagunços* gain the author's
implicit admiration and Antônio Conselheiro acquires
a heroic status. As Vargas Llosa himself has pointed out
in several interviews, Da Cunha was ultimately seduced by the beleaguered inhabitants of Canudos.
Consequently, everything that supposedly stood for the
opposite of civilization appealed to him most strongly.

Rebellion in the Backlands has several features
that would logically appeal to a writer like Vargas Llosa, if not openly "seduce" him. Vargas Llosa has always
been fascinated with the idea of the "total novel" to
which many great novelists aspire (see Chapter 7). The
translator's introduction to Da Cunha's book proposes
that *it* is just such a total work: "a complete psychological picture of the Brazilian soil, the people, and the
country, such as has never been achieved with equal
insight and psychological comprehension."[13] What
seems to have attracted Vargas Llosa most, however,

was this book as an adventure story. He has written of his attraction to the adventures of the novel of chivalry — above all, *Tirant lo Blanc* — and to such writers as Jules Verne and Alexandre Dumas. *Rebellion in the Backlands*, particularly in the final chapters, contains much of the human drama and sanguine violence that typifies the novel of chivalry in general and *Tirant lo Blanc* in particular. A description of the soldier's methods in torturing *jagunços* reads like many passages in the bloody *Tirant lo Blanc*:

That task, as we have seen, was a simple one. Fasten a leather tong around the victim's neck in the form of a halter or slip-knot, then drag him along between the rows of tents; no need to worry about anyone's being shocked by the procedure and no need to fear that the prey might escape, for, at the least sign of resistance or attempted flight, all one had to do was give a tug on the rope and the lasso would anticipate the work of the knife, and strangulation would take the place of beheading.[14]

Da Cunha's book was both a substantial source of information and catalyst for the creation of *The War of the End of the World*.

Plot and Structure

Whatever may be the historical or aesthetic merit of Da Cunha's tome, the more interesting matter for most contemporary readers, and especially for readers of Vargas Llosa, is his transformation of the anecdotal material of *Rebellion in the Backlands* into novelistic form in his novel. The original Spanish edition includes a full-page reproduction of a painting of "The Fanatic Antônio Conselheiro" — a kind of tribute to the priest and Da Cunha's popularization of him. Both the Spanish and English editions of *The War of the End of the World* contain a dedication "To Euclides Da Cunha." These are Vargas Llosa's only direct references to Da Cunha in the entire novel.

The War of the End of the World consists of four parts, each of which contains between three and seven chapters. Most chapters contain four or five brief narrative segments, usually three to eight pages in length. Part I (120 pages) has seven chapters, each with four narrative segments. Part II (11 pages) contains only three brief chapters, with no divisions into narrative segments. Part III (209 pages) offers seven chapters, each with five narrative segments. Part IV (215 pages) contains six chapters, each with four narrative segments. Although this may make the book appear similar in organization to *The Green House* or *Conversation in The Cathedral*, the novels are comparable in only the most superficial way: unlike the technically complex novels of the 1960s, *The War of the End of the World* is a basically straightforward narration related, for the most part, by a controlling omniscient narrator. In this sense it is Vargas Llosa's most traditional novel.

The plot does not engage the reader in the intricacies (and occasional difficulties) of multidimensional time or the juxtaposition of planes of reality, such as are found in his first three novels. *The War of the End of the World*, rather, overwhelms with the cumulative effect of seemingly endless detail and the intensity of human drama. In this sense it falls within the tradition of the great novelists of the nineteenth century, whom Vargas Llosa admires: Balzac and Tolstoy as examples.

Part I provides an introduction to most of the main characters, and to the general historical and political setting. By the end of Part I, the people of Canudos have stunned the government's soldiers by defeating the first two armies sent to the backlands to place the rebellious fanatics under control. The major characters introduced in Part I are Antônio Vicente Mendes Maciel (always called "the Counselor"), Galileo Gall, and Epaminondas Gonçalves. The narrator presents the Counselor as a special and extraordinary individual, portraying him as a living legend and, by the end of Part I, even Jesus-type figure.

His initial characterization features the mysterious background common in such figures: "It was impossible to learn his age, his background, his life story here, but there was something about his quiet manner, his frugal habits, his imperturbable gravity that attracted people even before he offered counsel."[15] He seems to have supernatural powers, gaining the "respect of rattlesnakes" and being spared the epidemics that appear regularly in the region. He publicly denounces the new Republic, criticizing, for example, the concept of taxes. When attacked by the police, his impoverished followers defend him.

Galileo Gall is a Scot, who arrived in Brazil shipwrecked. An anarchist revolutionary and phrenologist well before arriving in the New World, Gall is immediately attracted to the rebels' cause in Canudos. He writes letters to a European newspaper, *L'Étincelle de la Révolte*, about what he perceives as revolutionary idealism in Brazil. Gall hires a guide named Rufino to take him from Bahia to Canudos. During their trip they are attacked, Rufino escapes, and Gall, who has voluntarily abstained from any sexual activity for a decade, rapes Rufino's wife, Jurema. Epaminondas Gonçalves is the publisher of a newspaper of the region, the *Jornal de Notícias*. Even though his newspaper is pro-Republic and critical of the uprising in Canudos, Gonçalves and his colleagues of the Progressivist Republican Party contract Gall to deliver arms to the rebels. These Republican forces prefer to support the rebels in order to counterbalance the power of the landowners, an aristocracy represented by the Baron of Canabrava.

Part I also tells the story of a variety of characters who will eventually converge upon Canudos as dutiful followers of the Counselor. These outcasts include the Little Blessed One, Big João, Maria Quadrado, Antônio Vilanova, and León of Natuba. The Little Blessed One has been unable to fulfill his dream of becoming a priest because he was born out of wedlock. Moved by the Counselor's humble life, sage advice, and ability to predict the future, the Little Blessed One becomes one of his devout followers. The story of Big João is the most violent of Part I, and is representative of numerous passages of this sort in the novel. He is a black slave born as the result of his owner's careful selection of mates in order to "produce" an ideal physical specimen. As the narrator points out, the owner, Adalberto de Gumúcio, "dealt with his slaves in exactly the same way that he had dealt with his horses" (p. 25). Big João, after a privileged upbringing, and special care from De Gumúcio's sister, brutally attacks and kills her, lopping off her breasts and head. The pious and good-willed Maria Quadrado joins the Counselor's followers in Canudos after having been raped four times. The merchant Antônio Vilanova arrives in Canudos to become its most prosperous merchant, after fleeing a town plagued with an epidemic and repressed by local political bosses. An outcast named León of Natuba, a strange-looking creature born deformed with very short legs and an enormous head, is also taken in by the Counselor. In addition to this panoply of characters who will become the fierce and faithful of Canudos, Part I includes a government version of the situation: one narrative segment provides the account of the military officer Pires Ferreira's defeat in Canudos.

Following the introduction of the characters and the intensity of the military action in Part I — the two clashes between the inhabitants of Canudos and gov-

ernment soliders — Part II functions as a type of brief
interlude. One is afforded the opportunity to distance
himself from Canudos and view the situation as it is
seen through the press in Bahia (Salvador): The text of
an editorial appears in its entirety in the *Jornal de Notícias* on January 3, 1897. This text accuses the aristo-
cratic and conservative forces in Brazil of having col-
laborated with the English in fomenting the rebellion
in Canudos. Conversations between a newspaper em-
ployee identified only as a "nearsighted journalist" and
Gonçalves precede and follow this editorial prepared
by the myopic journalist.

Part III, like the third act of a traditional four-act
play, complicates the plot and intensifies the human
drama. Two characters who will have an enormous impact appear on the scene: Colonel Moreira César and
the Baron of Canabrava. Moreira César arrives at the
rural town of Queimadas as a hero of the Brazilian
Republic. A banner that awaits him proclaims: QUEIMA-
DAS WELCOMES HEROIC COLONEL MOREIRA CÉSAR AND
HIS GLORIOUS REGIMENT. LONG LIVE BRAZIL! Neither
he nor the citizens of the Republic have the slightest
doubt that he will save it from the fanatics in the
North. Much of Part III involves the slow advancement
of his troops upon Canudos and their positioning for
battle. From the point of view of the Baron of Canabrava, whom the reader observes discussing politics
with Adalberto de Gumúcio, the military represents a
threat to the power of the landed aristocracy: a military victory in Canudos could precipitate a sweep into
power. Consequently, one discovers that there are four
sources of power vying for potential control of Brazil:
the Counselor, the middle-class Republicans, the aristocracy, and the military.

Concomitant with this political and military maneuvering, the fanatics in Canudos busy themselves
with preparations to defend their town from the inevi-

table next attack. There are other side plots: Rufino searches for Gall in order to avenge the violation of his wife; Gall, Jurema, and a group of bizarre types belonging to a circus travel across the countryside toward Canudos. The conflicts intensify in both a general and more specific fashion: the *jagunços* raze the Baron of Canabrava's estate; Gall and Rufino kill each other in hand-to-hand combat. Part III ends with Moreira César's protracted and devastating defeat at the hands of the *jagunços*. The Baron of Canabrava and Gonçalves agree to collaborate now that Moreira César has been eliminated.

Part IV is dedicated almost entirely to the final siege on Canudos, which eventually destroys the *jagunços* and any remnants of the town. The first three chapters describe preparations for the siege and the beginnings of the battle. The last three chapters, functioning as a type of epilogue, relate, after the fact, what has happened in Canudos.

Even this brief plot résumé suggests several ways in which Vargas Llosa used Da Cunha's to tell the story of Canudos. The two most outstanding parallels are the characterizations of the Counselor and the Colonel Moreira César. Vargas Llosa *re*creates the two persons described by Da Cunha, changing certain details and allowing imagination to create others. For example, the purple tunic that drapes over the Counselor in *Rebellion in the Backlands* becomes a blue one in *The War of the End of the World*. Some of Da Cunha's dates and facts also filter into Vargas Llosa's text: the 5,200 dwellings from Da Cunha's documentation become a similar 5,783 in *The War of the End of the World*. Though the numbers are not identical, they respond to a similar impulse toward documentation. Other direct comparisons between the two texts can be made.[16]

The interesting relationship between the two books, however, is not to be found by comparing dwellings and such as they appear in Canudos. Rather, the general is more interesting than the specific in making comparisons: Da Cunha was an indefatigable investigator and Brazilian nationalist, who seemingly attempted to write the "total" Brazilian book; Vargas Llosa, on the other hand, resists the totalization impulse with this material. Da Cunha relates a plethora of facts and situations, but his book acquires the drama of a story only at the end; Vargas Llosa limits himself to telling numerous stories which, interwoven and experienced in their totality, are still an overwhelmingly powerful human drama. In this sense the Peruvian writer has selectively transformed a massive human circumstance into a complete and whole human story. The nearsighted journalist in *The War of the End of the World*, always awkward and inadequate, seems to play the role of Da Cunha the journalist: he haphazardly gets the information, but really fails to tell the story.

As in Vargas Llosa's previous novels, plot in itself is once again a predominant factor. The difficult element for the reader of this novel is the density and length of the story, rather than intercalated dialogues or complex relationships between fictional readers and writers. Narrative technique is not in itself such an explicit issue, and the effects of Vargas Llosa's techniques are more subtle than in his more overtly Faulknerian texts.

Theme and Technique

Some of Vargas Llosa's constant thematic concerns reappear in *The War of the End of the World*. The fanaticism that emanates from both Canudos and some Republicans has traces of the attitudes of a Pantaleón Pantoja or a Pedro Camacho. Once again Vargas Llosa exploits the humorous potential of fanaticism, although

the experience of this novel is predominantly tragic
rather than comic. Once again the novelist places in
question the potential of the purely rational in compre-
hending reality. Rather than questioning reality by un-
dermining it, as in *The Green House* and *Conversation
in The Cathedral*, in *The War of the End of the World*
the rational is called into question by means of the
characterization of Galileo Gall, who is one of the most
intellectual and rational, as well as one of the most
flagrant fools, of the novel. Gall confides early that
"there is no such thing as chance in history, that however fortuitous its course may seem, there is always a
rationality lying hidden behind even the most puzzling
appearances" (p. 83). The presence of the military,
most evident before in *The Time of the Hero* and *Captain Pantoja and the Special Service*, is once again ush-
ered forth as a central preoccupation.[17] The fanaticism,
rigidity, and stupidity of military figures in this novel
make them victims, once again, of Vargas Llosa's critical and occasionally satirical pen.

More comprehensive and penetrating thematic
schemes, however, subsume the issues mentioned
above. *The War of the End of the World* is essentially a
story of conflict; antagonistic forces come into contact
at various levels. The three most basic levels are: a conflict of ideologies; a conflict of individuals; and a conflict of languages. Although these levels are not mutually exclusive, they will be discussed separately here for
the sake of clarity.

The conflict of ideologies involves the four political forces in opposition: the middle-class Republicans,
the traditional aristocracy, the military, and the rebels
in Canudos. The Republicans represent the ideals of
constitutional democracies along the lines of those that
had been popularized with the revolutions in France
and the United States. Centuries of rule from Portu-
gal — in collaboration with the Brazilian aristocracy —

and the failure of many Latin American republics during the nineteenth century made the proposition of the new republic in Brazil a tenuous one indeed. The landed aristocracy represented more conservative positions than the Republicans, and its power was threatened with the rising power of the Republican party. A typical Latin American paradigm would include the institutions of the church and the military operating in conjunction. Here the conflict of ideologies takes a bizarre twist: the aristocracy (represented by the Baron of Canabrava), the rebels (represented by the Counselor and his *jagunços*), and the military (best epitomized by Moreira César) are antagonistic. The rebels, in turn, are an unorthodox combination of the working class, the unemployed, and the church.

As Raymond Souza has pointed out, the war of ideologies is played out by means of conflicts among the major characters.[18] The characterizations of the Counselor, Moreira César, and the Baron, are essential to the dynamics of the conflict. The Counselor not only practices and preaches his religion, but also appears as a Christ-figure throughout the novel. Whereas the Counselor's persona is spiritual, negating the material world, Moreira César is a materialist who believes in scientific progress. The Baron, like Moreira César, is a pragmatist but, unlike the Colonel, he does not allow idealism to interfere with his understanding of the mechanics of how things work. For this reason the Baron is the only character in the novel who would be capable of equating Gall with Moreira César. The Baron explains:

"The only thing I didn't understand was what pretext Epaminondas had used to attract the supposed agent to the backlands," he said, moving his fingers as though he had cramps in them. "It never entered my head that heaven might favor him by putting an idealist in his hands. A strange breed, idealists. I've never met one before, and now, in the space of just a few days, I've had dealings with two of them. The

other one is Colonel Moreira César. Yes, he too is a dreamer.
Though his dreams and yours don't coincide. . . . (p. 244)

The fight between Rufino and Gall is also a synecdoche
for a larger war and in this sense is an ideological battle.[19] Rufino represents the old and traditional; Gall,
the modern and revolutionary. Their mutual destruc-
tion is a simplified version of what happens in Canudos.

In some situations the conflicts of individuals sub-
vert an exclusively ideological understanding of the
events at hand. It has already been noted how the political becomes a backdrop rather than a predominant
motivating factor by the last part of *Conversation in
The Cathedral* (see Chapter 4). Personal motives also
negate a purely ideological reading of *The War of the
End of the World*. Characters are seen responding to
powerful — and also petty — human motives in situations in which the reader might well expect the general
ideological framework to be more operational. Gall's
political ideals and contradictions make him one of the
most interesting characters in this context. When Rufino approaches Gall with the intention of defending
the lost honor of his wife, Gall reacts with a political
response:

His [Gall's] feeling of unreality grew even more intense. He
raised his free hand and made a peaceable, friendly gesture.
"There's no time for this, Rufino. I can explain to you what
happened. There's something that's much more urgent now.
There are thousands of men and women who risk being killed
because of a handful of ambitious politicians. It's your
duty . . ." (p. 291).

Rufino, of course, is not capable of conceptualiz-
ing the situation in ideological terms. The often-
intellectual nearsighted journalist, more distant and
objective about the phenomena of northeastern Brazil

than most of its inhabitants, questions the conflict in a strictly ideological context. The narrator reveals the journalist's thoughts on the issue:

Can Canudos be explained in terms of the familiar concepts of conspiracy, rebellion, subversion, intrigues of politicians out to restore monarchy? Listening to that terrified little priest today, he has had the certainty that all that is not the explanation. Something more diffuse, timeless, extraordinary, something that his skepticism presents him from calling divine or diabolical or simply spiritual. What is it, then? He runs his tongue across the mouth of his empty canteen and a few moments later falls asleep (p. 258).

Even this intellectual character is not capable of formulating an all-encompassing response to the problem. Both the events and this type of questioning, however, lead the reader to conclude that the ideological conflict is only one level of an understanding of events that also relate to basic human drives and motives. Consequently, it is possible to find scenes in the novel in which the soldiers respond not to the nationalistic ideals for which they ostensibly are fighting, but rather to the most basic and petty needs: Private Queluz, for example, has homosexual fantasies and an erection while thinking of Captain Oliveira's orderly in the midst of a battle (pp. 526–32).

On a third level of conflict, *The War of the End of the World* relates an encounter of competing languages. Differences in class and ideology, as well as deep-seated cultural and religious traditions, make this novel rich in the multiple languages of a text which Bakhtin has identified as heteroglossia. Among the numerous languages present, the two that predominate are a medieval language of Christianity and a modern language of Enlightenment.

The language of Christianity permeates the novel and has multiple sources (such as the priests in the local villages), but emanates above all from the Counselor. And the narrator frequently uses this language when describing or referring to the Counselor. For example, the following passage is narrated by the omniscient narrator outside of the story and refers to the Counselor:

Lo verían esta tarde, en el Templo; lo oirían dar consejos y decirles que el Padre estaba dichoso de recibirlos en el rebaño. Los vio partir, aturdidos de gozo. Era purificadora la presencia de la gracia en este mundo condenado a la perdición.[20]

They would see him that evening, in the Temple; they would hear him give Counsel and tell them that the Father was happy to receive them into the flock. He saw them leave, giddy with joy. The presence of grace in this world doomed to perdition was purifying (p. 233).

The modern language of the Enlightenment is notably present in narrative segments dealing with nationalistic characters, such as Gonçalves and Moreira César. Gonçalves, for example, speaks of "democratic ideals"—an Enlightenment language long since appropriated and institutionalized by the constitutions of many American republics. The military language of the passages dealing with the officers sent to Canudos contains frequent traces of a political discourse that is also markably influenced by the Enlightenment. At times the use of this exaggerated military language is parodic and achieves humorous effects. *The War of the End of the World* contains less dialogue among characters than novels such as *The Green House, Conversation in The Cathedral*, or *Captain Pantoja and the Special Service*. Nevertheless, it is a truly "dialogic" text in the sense that Bakhtin has used the term: it is a dialogue among languages.[21]

With respect to narrative technique, on the sur-

face the novel seems traditional and even relatively simple. It is Vargas Llosa's only novel narrated extensively
and consistently by a traditional omniscient narrator
outside of the story. All of his previous novels feature a
multiplicity of speakers, most of whom are characters
within the story. In the first three novels, passages of a
traditional third-person narration are sparse, and they
are usually abundant in dialogue. One of the few exceptions to such a generalization are those passages early in
The Green House that describe Piura (see Chapter 3).

More specifically, there are four types of narrative
situations in this novel. The first and most common are
narrative segments told by an omniscient narrator outside the story.[22] The second narrative situation, of
which there are only two narrative segments in the
novel, is Gall's narrative, an account written for publication in the newspaper *L'Étincelle de la Révolte*. The
third narrative situation, similar but not identical to
the second, is a report written by the nearsighted journalist in the *Jornal de Noticias* (pp. 128–30). The
fourth narrative situation involves an omniscient narrator, but the fictional world is filtered through the eyes
of a character who functions as a seer or, to use a more
precise term, focaliser.[23]

The traditional omniscient narrator controls the
major portion of the novel. Some sections, particularly
early on, feature a camera-eye objectivity, or strictly
exterior presentation of the characters:

The lady pays, pockets the change, and as she leaves the
counter, the person waiting behind her moves forward and
hands the cashier a piece of paper. He is dressed in a black
frock coat and bowler that show signs of wear. Curly red
locks cover his ears. He is a full-grown man, on the tall side,
solidly built, with broad shoulders (pp. 6–7).

Despite a basic position of presenting characters in

an impersonal and exterior fashion, the narrator occasionally demonstrates more personal attitudes and a limited omniscience. The narrator characterizes Gall, for example, as follows: "Galileo Gall had apparently passed his examinations and was about to receive his medical degree when his love of freedom and progress, or his vocation as an adventurer, again impelled him to action and a life on the move" (p. 15). ["Parecía que se iba a recibir de médico cuando su amor a la libertad y el progreso o su vocación aventurera pusieron otra vez en movimiento su vida." (p. 25)]. The knowledge revealed here is not one of total omniscience: the narrator is not sure what Gall's motives were for becoming a man of action (ideals or adventure). Moreover, the act of proposing these two possibilities suggests a cynical attitude on the narrator's part with respect to Gall. By questioning Gall's ideals, the narrator reveals an implied attitude about the Scottish adventurer.

The narrator's treatment of the Counselor consistently involves a distanced perspective that is never totally omniscient. According to the narrator, for example, the Counselor "scarcely appeared to be aware of the human trail tagging along after him" (p. 16) ["parecía apenas darse cuenta de la estela humana que prolongaba sus huellas." (p. 27)] Much of what the narrator reveals about the Counselor, in fact, deals with how he "appears," rather than, for example, what he truly is or thinks. Consequently, the reader views the Counselor in a fashion similar to how a person in Canudos might, with no special or privileged knowledge. Along these lines, the omniscient narrator assumes the role of communicator of popular legend ("Legend had it that . . ." [p. 116]) and rumor.

The function of Gall's letters to *L'Étincelle de la Révolte* and the newspaper article in the *Jornal de Noticias* is to afford the reader a broader vision of the events at hand than is possible in individual characterizations or even group situations. Gall's letters offer a very particular interpretation of events: that of an anarchist revolutionary writing to an audience of similar beliefs. The article in *Jornal de Noticias* is written by a Republican (the nearsighted journalist) to an assumed readership of the same party. The letters and articles are the broadest vision the reader will have of strictly political events.

The fourth type of narrative situation, with an omniscient narrator and a character or characters who function as focaliser(s), is similar to several key passages in *Conversation in The Cathedral* (see Chapter 4). The technique is far more important to the experience of *The War of the End of the World* than the apparently traditional format of the novel might initially suggest. In many of the narrative segments with an omniscient narrator the "seer" is the figure of the narrator himself; this is the most prevalent mode of narration in Part I. A few of the narrative segments in Part I, however, present the fictional world partially through the eyes of one or more other characters. For example, the end of Big João's story (pp. 25–30) features him as focaliser, and the following segment dealing with Gall has Van Rijsted as focaliser. Four other narrative segments in Part One have focalisers who are characters — two with Gall as sole focaliser (pp. 52–56 and pp. 110–14), another with Gonçalves and Gall as focalisers (pp. 72–74), and a fourth with Jurema and Gall who function as focalisers (pp. 89–94).

In Part II and Part III of the novel there is even more division between an omniscient narrator who is the seer and characters who are focalisers. Of the thirty-eight narrative segments in these two parts of the novel, in sixteen the omniscient narrator is the "seer" and twenty-two have characters who function as focalisers. By Part IV *each* of the twenty-four narrative segments has a character who is the focaliser — all of the

final events are presented to the reader through the eyes
of characters. These focalisers appear as follows:

Part IV
I. 1. Baron of Canabrava
2. Abbot João
3. Nearsighted journalist
4. Pires Ferreira
II. 1. Baron of Canabrava
2. Pajeú
3. Jurema
4. Medrado
III. 1. Nearsighted journalist
2. Big João
3. Dwarf
4. Calvalcanti
IV. 1. Baron of Canabrava
2. Vilanova
3. Nearsighted journalist
4. General Artur Oscar
V. 1. Baron of Canabrava
2. Little Blessed One
3. Jurema
4. Private Queluz
VI. 1. Baron of Canabrava
2. Lion of Natuba
3. Dwarf
4. Colonel Macedo

This extensive use of characters as focalisers in Part IV
makes the experience of this entire section qualitatively
different from the entire previous sections of the novel,
and markedly different from Part I. Part IV is characterized by the intensity and closeness of the experience
of Canudos's final downfall, as literally seen by characters on both sides of the ideological and physical war.

There is also considerable variation in verb tense

throughout the novel, alternating between present and past. Of the ninety-one narrative segments in the novel, thirty-seven take place in the present and fifty-one are in the past (the three remaining are Gall's two letters and a newspaper article). The narrative segments in the first three parts of the novel that have characters as focalisers are narrated predominantly, but not exclusively, in the present tense. For example, in Part III the characters who function as focalisers are Rufino (pp. 156–61, 184–87, 207–10, 238–43, 270–77), Moreira César (168–74), Moreira César and the nearsighted journalist (192–99, 218–24), Little Blessed One (232–38), Baron of Canabrava (243–51), the nearsighted journalist (251–60, 284–90, 312–22, 337–44), Gall (260–65), Lion of Natuba (265–70), Maria Quadrado (297–304), Jurema (304–8, 322–28), and Antônio Vilanova (328–37). Of these twenty narrative segments with characters as focalisers, only six are in the past tense. The passages in the present communicate a sense of immediacy for the reader in both time and space. In Part IV, twelve of the total twenty-four narrative segments are narrated in the present tense and twelve are in the past.

The novel's most noteworthy "seer" is the nearsighted journalist. He not only appears in nine narrative segments as focaliser, but also functions as a Da Cunha–type character who provides the reader with a journalist's "firsthand account" of the events at Canudos. As a newspaperman charged with getting the complete story, the journalist is the seer par excellence. He first appears as focaliser in a narrative segment in which he shares the seeing with Moreira César (Part III, Chapter 3, pp. 192–99). In the opening paragraphs of this narrative segment Moreira César is the focaliser: the reader is cognizant of the situation within the limits of what Moreira César perceives. The reader is privy to

what this officer sees, hears, and thinks. Later in this
narrative segment the focalisation moves to the journalist, first by indicating what he thinks: "'Is this what
war is?' the nearsighted journalist thinks" (p. 194).
["'¿Esta es la guerra?' piensa el periodista miope." (p.
192)]. Later in this narrative segment, the journalist
functions as the reader's seer:

El periodista del *Jornal de Noticias* va a sentarse también,
cuando ve a Moreira César llevarse las manos a la cara. Su
quepis cae al suelo y el Coronel se levanta de un brinco y
comienza a dar traspiés, congestionado, mientras se arranca
a manotazos los botones de la camisa, como si se ahogara (p.
194).

The reporter from the *Jornal de Noticias* goes over and sits
down, too, when he *sees* Moreria César raise his hands to his
face. The colonel's kepi falls to the ground and he leaps to his
feet, staggering, his face beet-red, as he frantically rips off
the buttons of his blouse, as though suffocating (my emphasis, p. 196).

In passages such as this the reader's perception of Moreira César's actions is filtered through the nearsighted
journalist as focaliser.

A key passage for the nearsighted journalist — and
quite likely one of the most memorable passages of the
novel — takes place near the conclusion of Part III,
when he views Canudos after a devastating battle
(Chapter 7, pp. 337–44). This passage begins with a
series of sensations as perceived by the nearsighted journalist: "In that dreaming that is and is not, a dozing
that blurs the borderline between waking and sleeping
and that reminds him of certain opium nights in his
disorderly little house in Salvador, the nearsighted cor-
respondent from the *Jornal de Noticias* has the sen-
sation that he has not slept but has spoken and
listened . . ." (p. 337). After a lengthy paragraph of
confusion and questioning on the nearsighted journal-

ist's part, the world literally comes into focus for him and for the reader:

He feels someone shaking him. He thinks: "My glasses." He sees a faint greenish light, moving shadows. And he pats his body, he feels all about him, he hears Father Joaquim. "Wake up, it's already light, let's try to find the road to Cumbe." He finally locates them, between his legs, unbroken. He cleans them, stands up, stammers "All right, all right," as he puts his glasses on and the world comes into focus he sees the Dwarf: a real one, as small as a ten-year-old boy with a face furrowed with wrinkles (p. 338).

Then the journalist travels with the Dwarf and Father Joaquim, eventually reaching a rocky crest line from which they can view (with the reader) a confrontation between the *jagunços* and masses of soldiers. Individual *jagunços* and soldiers come into focus for several pages as the journalist observes the maneuverings that take place in the scene below. He nears the battleground and experiences (above all, *sees*) the fighting in near-proximity (see p. 343). Near the end of the passage the fighting becomes intense and the narrator relates it exactly as the nearsighted journalist sees:

He *sees* as he passes by that *jagunços* are hanging kepis, tunics . . . And when, as they descend toward the sea of rooftops and rubble that is Canudos, he *sees* heads of dead soldiers lined up on either side of the trail . . . and he *recognizes* the naked, corpulent form . . . *he takes a close look* at one of the heads crawling with flies. There is no possible doubt: it is the head of Moreira César (my emphasis, p. 344).

Here Vargas Llosa has achieved a maximum impact in the culminating scene of Part III by using the journalist as focaliser. At this point, both the chaos of war and the emotional impact of its savagery have reached an apex and breaking point. Consequently, it seems only appropriate that the journalist (and the reader) see no more: the journalist's glasses break, and when he puts them on again he finds himself "Looking out at a shattered, cracked, crazed world" (p. 344). This narrative segment ends as follows: "He feels in his right hand a hand that — from its size, from its pressure — can only be that of the barefoot woman. She pulls him along, without a word, guiding him in this world suddenly become inapprehensible, blind" (p. 344). Without his glasses the journalist is thrust into a world of vague sensations, just as this narrative segment had begun — before he put his glasses on.

By using a focaliser in this fashion Vargas Llosa has made one of the key events in the novel not only a turning point in the development of the plot but also a unique and direct experience for the reader. The reader has had the privilege of experiencing the horror of Canudos not vicariously, but as co-participant with the nearsighted journalist.

The use of focalisers contributes to another of Vargas Llosa's most effective, albeit standard, narrative techniques: the presentation of two versions, or sides, of the same story. In *The War of the End of the World*, of course, there are basically two groups in conflict as far as the physical combat is concerned, and Vargas Llosa presents both sides in the same intimate detail. Da Cunha had begun his account of the Canudos conflict by describing adversaries such as Big João and Moreira César; the Brazilian author then associated himself with the government soldiers ("our troops," as he calls them), only to become enchanted, in the end, with the *jagunços'* heroism. Vargas Llosa consistently seems to take both sides. Throughout the novel there are characters who appear as focalisers on both sides of the war. Part IV, especially, gives the reader a constantly changing point of view on the events at hand, from characters actually on both sides of the battlefield to such distant observers as the Baron.

Vargas Llosa's use of the language of both sides is

one of the most effective means of underlining the real differences and the false differences — misunderstandings — between the two groups. The people of Canudos always use the term "Throat Slitter" whenever they refer to the character known to the reader and to outsiders to Canudos as Moreira César, patriot and hero. The inhabitants of Canudos appear in their narrative segments as poverty-stricken and religious, yet in those narrative segments focusing on the military they are the "English" and "Freemasons." Neither side even questions this contradictory language. In this way, through language itself, the reader becomes aware of the enormous distance between the two enemies. This use of different language for different groups communicates to the reader precisely what Vargas Llosa has said about the historical events in Canudos: both sides were fighting ghosts that were the product of their respective imaginations. The near-sighted journalist arrives at this conclusion: "It's not so much a story of madmen as a story of misunderstandings" (p. 461).

A Novel of Synthesis

Vargas Llosa has been characterized from his early work as a technician and storyteller. If *Conversation in The Cathedral* is the final step of his development as a master of technique, *The War of the End of the World* is the culmination of his production as a storyteller. This novel also represents a synthesis of other specific themes and techniques from his previous work.

In addition to retelling Da Cunha's story of Canudos as has been delineated above, Vargas Llosa relates countless associated stories. In such works as *The Green House* and *Aunt Julia and the Script Writer* he used formal structures to incorporate a multiplicity of stories. Even though *The War of the End of the World* offers a more traditional presentation of the anecdotal material, Vargas Llosa does use the Canudos story to relate individual and virtually self-sufficient stories similar to many of those of his previous books.

One narrative segment in Part IV, for example, tells the story of Frutuoso Medrado, a sergeant in the Republican army. It is an eight-page section that relates his entire story; he has no significant role in the novel before or after this narrative segment. Medrado is the focaliser and the entire anecdote is related in the present tense. The reader is able to observe Medrado as he contemplates the "English" enemy he believes he is fighting. His thoughts as a military officer recall *Captain Pantoja and the Special Service* and evoke similar humorous responses. Unable to understand the logic of a command given, he "thinks to himself that one of the few disadvantages of his military life that he relishes so is the mysterious nature of certain command decisions" (pp. 407–8). As he observes the enemy and his colleagues, Medrado sees Private Corintio nearby and says to himself: "What a hot bitch you are, Florissa — here I am, miles away in the middle of a war, and still you've made me get a hard-on" (p. 409). ["Qué puta eres, Florissa, piensa. Qué puta para que, estando tan lejos y en una guerra, seas capaz de parármela" (p. 388)]. The battle intensifies and, being the traditional military man that he is, Medrado relies on military maxims for assurance: "A wasted bullet weakens the one who wastes it; shoot only when you can see what you're shooting at" (p. 411). He also recites from the *Official Rule Books of Tactics* with the military rigidity that achieves the humorously ridiculous already observed in *Captain Pantoja and the Special Service*. The story ends as a personal melodrama worthy of one of Pedro Camacho's melodramas in *Aunt Julia and the Script Writer*. Medrado is wounded and begs for Private Corintio's assistance: "Florissa's husband is plunging his bayonet into his neck beneath the revolted gaze of the other one, whom Frutuoso Medrado also recognizes: Argimiro. He manages to say to himself that Corintio did know, after all" (p. 415).

Medrado does participate in the flow of the Canudos story. Nevertheless, this anecdote could almost function as a self-sufficient story. Indeed, one source of humor, and the success of this anecdote as a story, derives from elements unrelated to the conflict in Canudos. Medrado's story is one of the more entertaining individual anecdotes of the novel, but certainly not the only one of this type.

Storytelling is also of thematic importance in this novel. The conflict Vargas Llosa has set forth is that of an encounter between the forces of oral and written culture.[24] The oral culture is that of the Counselor, who constantly tells stories (mostly anecdotes of Biblical tradition). Indeed, he becomes a legend because of the stories that others tell of him. The Counselor's thousands of followers in Canudos, most of whom are illiterate, are willing to sacrifice their lives because they see their existence and sacrifices as part of a larger story that the Counselor has so masterfully related, and that his most able followers relate for him. In conflict with this oral culture of storytellers is a written culture, which places its ultimate authority not in a verbally related story, but in a written constitution and written laws; the military that emanates from this (written) Republic is also a predominantly written culture, as Sergeant Medrado demonstrates when reciting from his *Official Rule Book of Tactics*.

One important reason for conflict between the Counselor and the Republic is that the written culture imposed on Canudos — from the very idea of a Republic to its taxes — is basically incomprehensible to an oral culture such as that of this town in northeastern Brazil. The Counselor's story would probably be comprehensible to those of the other side, but it remains unheard. Since communication between these two cultures, and qualitatively different stories, was impossible the only recourse was speculation. The verbal culture correctly named Moreira César "Throat Slitter"; the written culture incorrectly identified the *jagunços* as "English." The misnomers and misinformation can multiply because it is unrestrained, since each story — the verbal one and the written — is circumscribed by mutually exclusive boundaries.

Like *The Time of the Hero*, *The Green House*, and *Conversation in The Cathedral*, *The War of the End of the World* develops characters who function as part of a network of human relationships. The novel abounds in characters, and they all eventually not only relate to the whole, but survive or die as part of the network. Several characters, such as the Little Blessed One and Maria Quadrado, gain their only humanity by means of their relationship with the Counselor. They also perish as part of a human grouping that has been bonded by the Counselor's story. As in the previous novels, characters seem to relate to each other in ways that are sometimes surprisingly coincidental. These paradoxes reaffirm Vargas Llosa's vision of how individual acts affect the whole, and vice versa.

Fanaticism is one factor that motivates characters in *The War of the End of the World*, although it is not the predominant one. By dealing with fanaticism Vargas Llosa has continued to explore a facet of human behavior fictionalized in the character of Father García of *The Green House*, Captain Pantoja, and Pedro Camacho of *Aunt Julia and the Script Writer*. He brings fanatic attitudes to the realm of contemporary politics in Peru with a more recent novel, *The Real Life of Alejandro Mayta*.

7

Essays, Theater, and
The Real Life of
Alejandro Mayta (1984)

Vargas Llosa's most substantive production has been his
fiction, and any study of his complete work must give a
central role to his novels. He has also distinguished
himself, however, as a literary scholar, essayist, journalist, and playwright. This activity underlines Vargas
Llosa's versatility and prolificacy. In numerous essays
and interviews he has emphasized the writer's responsibility to society, in the tradition of Sartre and generations of Latin American writers. Consequently, Vargas
Llosa has articulated well-defined positions on a panoply of literary, social, and political issues. Some of his
nonfiction is of exceptional quality. Some of the essays,
dealing with topics of only transitory interest, are more
attractive to a general readership simply for having
been penned by Vargas Llosa; they contribute to the
total portrait of an intellectual actively involved in his
professional and social role in the Hispanic world.

Vargas Llosa's most significant literary scholarship
has appeared in the form of two book-length studies,
one on García Márquez and the other on Flaubert's
Madame Bovary. A compilation of previously published literary and political essays appeared in a volume entitled *Contra viento y marea* (Against Wind and
Nausea; 1983). He has also published two plays and,

most recently, a novel which, like many of his essays, is a contemplation on the recent political scene in
Peru.

Essays

The essays are those of a traditionalist disinterested, for
the most part, in recent theoretical developments of
structuralist and post-structuralist thought, and sometimes openly disapproving of the critical enterprise as it
is presently being practiced. He also has traditional
preferences in the novel, lauding the nineteenth-century European masters of the craft of fiction. Among his
"best friends" he lists fictional characters such as d'Ar-
tagnan, David Copperfield, Jean Valjean, Pierre Be-
zukhov, and Fabrizio del Dougo—certainly not a list
to be confused with the avant-garde of contemporary
writing. He also has written so regularly about his fascination with medieval novels of chivalry that he has
contributed to the popularizing of the genre in the Hispanic world.[1] By contrast, few contemporary Latin
American writers would agree with Vargas Llosa's critical attitude toward the French *nouveau roman*.

   In many of his journalistic essays, and in his study
of *Madame Bovary*, Vargas Llosa reveals much about
his personal literary tastes and interests. It is not surprising that he prefers books with "rigorous and sym-
metrical structure."[2] He unabashedly admits to other
rather mundane requisites for the novels he reads with
pleasure: rebellion, violence, and sex.[3] (These four characteristics, delineated by Vargas Llosa in 1975, are
practically a complete formula for the novel *The War
of the End of the World* he would publish six years
later.) To him novels without violence seem unreal. His
fascination with the melodramatic has its roots, he

claims, in the Mexican films that are popular throughout the Hispanic world. Sometimes Vargas Llosa can be
self-consciously analytical about such tendencies:
" . . . melodrama moves me because melodrama is
closer to the real."[4] With respect to sex, he is "as irritat-
ed by a novel that omits sexual experience as by one
that reduces life exclusively to the sexual."[5]

Vargas Llosa's ideas on fiction are less an abstract
theory of the novel than a pragmatic description of the
basic principles of storytelling. These principles have a
Vargas Llosa trademark primarily because they are his
own very personal selection of narrative procedures,
and they are described by him in consistently dramatic
and even volatile terms: he speaks of a writer's "personal demons," and of writing as an "act of rebellion
against God."

Many of his tenets as a writer, which have appeared in various forms in essays and interviews, are set
forth in a section entitled "The Novelist and His Demons" in his book on García Márquez:

To write novels is an act of rebellion against reality, against
God, against creation, which is reality. It is an attempt to
correct, charge, or abolish real reality, substituting for it the
fictional reality which the novelist creates. He is a dissident:
he creates an illusory life, he creates verbal worlds because he
doesn't accept life and the world as they are (or as he thinks
they are). At the root of his vocation is a feeling of dissatisfac-
tion about life; each novel is a secret deicide, a symbolic as-
sassination of reality.[6]

Rebellion, dissidence, and deicide are constant themes
in Vargas Llosa's literary essays. Later in the same
chapter he speaks more specifically of "demons," delin-
eating "personal demons," "historical demons," and
"cultural demons." The "personal demons" that incite
the writer to create are those personal experiences that
affect the potential novelist. "Historical demons" are

facts of a social nature that play a role in one's writing.
Reading and other cultural background form the "cultural demons" that can play a role in an author's creation. Vargas Llosa's discussions of fiction also refer regularly to what he calls the "added element" of any
novel: "This *added element* is what makes any novel a
work of creation and not of information, that which we
appropriately call the originality of a novelist."[7]

Vargas Llosa's first book-length exercise in practical criticism was *García Márquez: historia de un deicidio* (1971), (García Márquez: Story of a Deicide) a 667-
page study of that writer's life and the complete works
published to that date. In addition to being the most
comprehensive study at that time on García Márquez,
it functioned as a platform to set forth Vargas Llosa's
own principles of fiction. The first of ten parts consists
of an authoritative biography of García Márquez, a
seventy-one-page overview of the Colombian writer's
life from his birth in the 1920s to his life as the celebrated author of *One Hundred Years of Solitude* in the late
1960s. Part II, "The Writer and His Demons," offers the
general concepts discussed above, and applies them
specifically to García Márquez. The remaining eight
parts are analyses of García Márquez's complete work
from his first stories published in newspapers in the late
1940s to *One Hundred Years of Solitude* (1967).

The most substantive contribution of this book is
the detailed analysis of *One Hundred Years of Solitude*,
in which Vargas Llosa sets forth the concept of the
"total novel," which he has popularized in the Hispanic
world. The analysis is divided into three sections: (1) "A
Total Material," (2) "A Total Form," (3) "The Narrative
Strategy." The first two sections are an elaboration of
the idea of *One Hundred Years* as a total novel; the
third part is close analysis of its narrative technique.

One Hundred Years of Solitude is a total novel,
according to Vargas Llosa, for several reasons. It falls in

line with those ambitious creations that can compete with "real reality," confronting this reality with a vitality, vastness, and complexity that are qualitatively equivalent. This totality manifests itself above all in the plural nature of the novel, which represents, simultaneously, elements that had been considered antagonistic: traditional and modern, local and universal, imaginary and realist.⁸ Another aspect of its "totality" is its unlimited access: *One Hundred Years of Solitude* is within the reach of all readers and will offer different rewards for different types of reading. But García Márquez's grandiose work is a total novel above all because it puts into practice the utopian plan of all God's replacement-figures: to describe a total world, to confront "real reality" with an image that is both its expression and negation.⁹ It is a total novel with respect to content because it includes all the planes or levels of life of the fictional world. It is a total novel because it is a self-sufficient and autonomous verbal construct.

Vargas Llosa's analysis of García Márquez's narrative technique is a minute exercise in close reading. He examines such matters as the relationship between the narrator and that which is narrated, circular time, numerous episodes that close upon themselves, the counterpoint between the "real objective" and the "real imaginary" (in his terminology), and other matters related to the Colombian writer's narrative strategies. Among the techniques Vargas Llosa describes, always with a detailed set of examples, are exaggeration, enumeration, rhetorical symmetry, and repetition.

Vargas Llosa's other book-length critical study is *La orgía perpetua: Flaubert y "Madame Bovary"* (The Perpetual Orgy: Flaubert and *Madame Bovary*). In his prefatory remarks Vargas Llosa proposes that there are three basic types of criticism: personal subjective, scientific and analytical, and historical. He then contin-

ues by explaining that his study of *Madame Bovary*
contains these three approaches: Part I is Vargas Llosa's
own personal account of his relationship with Flaubert's novel; Part II is his analysis of the text; Part III
deals with *Madame Bovary* in the context of literary
history.

Part I is the story of Vargas Llosa's passionate affair with *Madame Bovary*. He relates every memory he
has of the book, including a seemingly enchanted reading in Paris. Totally absorbed by Flaubert's novel in a
little room in the Hôtel Wetter, he read through the
afternoon and evening and saw the sun rise with the
book still in his hands. He fell asleep in the morning
and awoke with two realizations: that he wished he
were Flaubert and that he would be forever in love
with Emma Bovary. Having established his passion for
this novel, he then analyzes his emotional attraction to it,
and discovers his personal tastes described earlier in this
chapter: his preference for works of rigorous and symmet-
rical structure, his attraction to melodrama, etc.

Part II consists of Vargas Llosa's literary analysis of
the novel, which includes formal questions of the text,
such as "What were the literary sources of *Madame
Bovary*?" or "In what way was Flaubert's personal life
projected into *Madame Bovary*?" together with Vargas
Llosa's response. The second half of Part II contains
analysis of substitution techniques in Flaubert's novel
and commentary on different uses of time and changes
in the narrator's position. In Part III Vargas Llosa discusses *Madame Bovary* as the first "modern novel," discussing its form, its use of interior monologue and other
narrative techniques; and he compares Flaubert to Ber-
tolt Brecht.

These studies of García Márquez and Flaubert are eru-
dite contributions to the body of critical work on
these two authors. They are significant in the context of

Vargas Llosa's total work by their transformation of
critical analysis into story. The study on García Márquez is, above all, the story of that author's deicide.
The study of *Madame Bovary* is, in addition to literary
scholarship, the story of a Peruvian writer's passionate
affair with a French novel. The presentation of these
two scholarly books as story evinces Vargas Llosa's vocation as a storyteller; the result is two books of interest
not only to literary scholars, but also to the reading
public in the Hispanic world.[10]

Vargas Llosa's prefaces to books reflect concerns
similar to those of his book-length essays. He has published a twenty-one-page essay in Spanish entitled
"Martorell and the 'Added Element' in *Tirant lo Blanc*"
that is a preface to an edition of the letters of the Cata-
lonian writer Joanot Martorell, the author of that medieval novel of chivalry.[11] In this essay Vargas Llosa
reconfirms his enthusiasm for adventure, and becomes
intimately involved with the subtleties and details of
the medieval duels. He reads in Martorell characteristics identical to those he admired in García Márquez:
Martorell is a "dissident," a "blind rebel," and a "substi-
tute for God." An analysis of these letters also leads to
commentary on the particularity of Martorell's writing. Vargas Llosa sees in the Catalan's love for form — a
privileging of ritual and ceremony over substance — a
world "where appearance, gestures and formulas constitute the essence of life, the intimate keys to man's
conduct."[12] In his conclusion, Vargas Llosa returns to
one of his standard concepts of the writer's task:
" . . . at the same time that he [Martorell] told of life,
he contradicted it."[13] This conclusion underlines Vargas
Llosa's vision of a writer who rebels against reality and,
in a way, adjusts or corrects it according to personal
experience or the "demons" described in his study of
García Márquez.

Vargas Llosa's political essays are generally brief,

incisive, and directed to contemporary issues of vital importance for the Latin American intellectual. Such essays on political and cultural issues have appeared with regularity since the early 1960s in newspapers and magazines of the Hispanic world, sixty-four of which have been compiled in a volume entitled *Contra viento y marea* (Against Wind and Nausea; 1983). Defining and defending political stances can be difficult in any society, but the problem is especially acute in Latin America. On the surface, Vargas Llosa has undergone a political transformation: the revolutionary of the early 1960s becomes considerably more moderate by the early 1980s. As already suggested (see Chapter 1), however, it is possible to observe a consistent line of thought from the mid-1960s to 1971 that demonstrates his change of position from strict adherence to socialist principles to rupture with all authoritarian governments, including Marxist regimes. His consistency lies in his vigorous defense of basic human rights, above all freedom of expression. Many of these essays, such as those criticizing policies of the Cuban and Soviet-bloc governments, have not gained him favor among Latin American intellectuals of the left.

His other essays include commentary on writers such as Camus and Sartre, reviews, and background into the creative process involved in fabricating his own novels. In 1981 he published a book of essays on Sartre and Camus, *Entre Sartre y Camus* (Between Sartre and Camus), a collection of twelve essays that had appeared in newspapers and journals over a twenty-year period. As Vargas Llosa himself points out in the prologue, these essays say more about who wrote them than they do about Sartre, Camus, or Simone de Beauvoir.[14] Seen in their totality, these writings are laden with both contradictions and repetitions. Vargas Llosa justifies their publication "to show the itinerary of a Latin American who did his intellectual apprenticeship overwhelmed by Sartre's intelligence and dialectical vacillations and ended up embracing Camus's libertarian reformism."[15] Among his writings on the creative process and how his novels acquired their final form, his *Historia secreta de una novela* — about *The Green House* — is typical. It reveals the first experiences that would lead to the project, the research included, and how the book developed and changed during the writing process (see Chapter 3 for a more lengthy discussion of this essay within the context of the *The Green House*). Vargas Llosa conscientiously avoids explaining his novels to his readers. Nevertheless, essays related to his own novels, as well as many of them on other writers, do operate as a codification of his intentions.

Theater

"Theater interested me from a very early age," Vargas Llosa recalled in 1984. "I believe my first literary vocation was that of playwright. At least one of the first more or less serious things that I wrote was theater."[16]

Indeed, he had written his first play, the unexceptional *La huida del Inca* (The Flight of the Inca) when still in high school. Three decades later, he would realize his childhood desire of becoming a dramatist by publishing two plays, *La señorita de Tacna* (1981) (The Missus from Tacna) and *Kathie y el hipopótamo* (1983) (Kathie and the hippopotamus).

The plays have been performed throughout the Hispanic world. *La señorita de Tacna* premiered in the theater capital of Latin America, Buenos Aires, in May 1981. Later it was presented in Chile, Uruguay, Spain, Costa Rica, Nicaragua, and Madrid. *Kathie y el hipopótamo* has also had several performances since its premier in Caracas in April 1983. Vargas Llosa has seen some of these performances and has commented that "the interesting thing is to see how a play is above all a possiblility: it can metamorphose itself into something quite different to the extent that the intermediaries, the director, the actors, the choreographers, and technicians integrate elements as creative as the text itself."[17]

La señorita de Tacna is a two-act play dealing with aging, the family, pride, and individual destiny — according to the author.[18] It also confronts a more comprehensive topic: how and why stories are born. In Vargas Llosa's prefatory remarks he asks the question "Why does man need to tell stories?"

The principal characters are an aged spinster named Mamaé and her great-nephew, Belisario, a writer in his forties or fifties. The staging is fundamental to the plot: a division of the stage into two halves is the setting for the two main story lines. On one side is the modest middle-class apartment of Mamaé's grandparents, located in Lima during the 1950s. The other half of the stage is Belisario's study, located "anywhere in the world in the year 1980." It is a typical little study, with a desk, lots of papers, and a typewriter. Belisario's scenery is simple and realistic. The other setting, however, is unrealistic because it exists as Belisario's memory and changes to other places and time periods: the home where the Grandmother and Mamaé lived as children in Tacna (a town in southern Peru), another home in Arequipa (a city in southern Peru), and a house in Bolivia. Belisario remembers anecdotes from the family's life, and occasionally interacts with characters on the other half of the stage. These anecdotes relate the stories of Mamaé's failure in marriage with a Chilean military officer, the proud family's growing economic difficulties, and, finally, Mamaé's death.

Kathie y el hipopótamo is another two-act play related to the act of storytelling. The manner in which stories and characters are in constant transformation make any résumé of the plot a questionable undertaking. The two main characters, Kathie Kennety and Santiago Zavala, are accompanied by Ana de Zavala (Santiago's wife) and Juan, who play out roles according to the situations created by Kathie and Santiago. The entire story takes place in Kathie's *"buhardilla de Paris"* (always in quotation marks in the text; her "Parisian apartment" is located in Lima). Santiago is a humble professor and journalist who, in Kathie's apartment, narrates the story of exotic African adventures into a tape recorder. He also plays the role of Mark Griffin, a brilliant professor and handsome lover. Kathie, too, takes on a series of different roles, both as lover and wife. Kathie and Santiago are aided by Juan and Ana in carrying out these scenes, some of a past remembered or invented by Kathie and Santiago.

Vargas Llosa's Theater in the Context of His Fiction

These two plays have been reasonably well received on their aesthetic merits in much of the Hispanic world. Within the body of Vargas Llosa's total work, however, they are less substantive than his novels and of interest largely within the context of his fiction. Even a passing familiarity with the plays will recall characters and situations from the novels: Santiago Zavala from *Conversation in The Cathedral*, Pedro Camacho from *Aunt Julia and the Script Writer*, journalists, writers, and many of the frustrations and failures of Peruvian life suffered by characters from *The Time of the Hero* to *The War of the End of the World* (the latter published after these plays). Beyond these obvious points of contact, there are more significant confluences of Vargas Llosa's fiction and theater.

Most of Vargas Llosa's fiction contains elements of

the theater. Mention has been made of the development
of conflict in *Captain Pantoja and the Special Service*
and *The War of the End of the World* as in a traditional
play. Four of Vargas Llosa's major novels — *The Time of
the Hero, The Green House, Conversation in The Cathedral,* and *Captain Pantoja and the Special Service* —
are highly dialogic. *Conversation in The Cathedral*
represented Vargas Llosa's most elaborate fabrication
of a novel of dialogue; *Captain Pantoja and the Special
Service* has only a few narrative segments that are not
dialogue. Given this preference for using direct dialogue to narrate a story, it is hardly surprising that Vargas Llosa would ultimately turn to the artistic form of
pure dialogue: the theater.

Characters and situations in Vargas Llosa's early
fiction undergo constant transformations. As has been
discussed in the analyses of *The Time of the Hero* and
The Green House (see Chapters 2 and 3), reality in
these novels is in perpetual flux. The sergeant of the
Amazon in *The Green House,* for example, is transformed into Lituma when he is in Piura. The reality of
several characters in this novel, above all Anselmo's, is
subject to transformation according to the time period
of his life and the person telling the story. Vargas Llosa
creates similar experiences of transformation in the two
plays.

In *La señorita de Tacna* the stage and scenery are
arranged to facilitate transformations similar to those
described above in Vargas Llosa's fiction. The division
of the stage into two halves allows the audience to visu-
alize changes from the present to the past as the story
line flows from one time period to another. The first
transformation of this type occurs early in Act I, when
Belisario begins to speak and write, and Joaquin appears concurrently as a character from the past. More
important, Mamaé of the present transforms into
Elvira of the past — a change in name identical to this

procedure in Vargas Llosa's fiction. Belisario the storyteller also undergoes transformation as a participant in
the story: in Act I he plays the role of a little boy, asking
questions at Mamaé's feet (pp. 56–58); in Act II he
assumes the role of a priest in another scene with Mamaé (pp. 96–102).

    Kathie y el hipopótamo is an exercise in constant
transformation. Kathie and Santiago transform into
other characters, and Ana and Juan asssist in their
playing out their roles. At the beginning of Act I, for
example, Kathie changes into an adolescent chatting on
a street corner with Juan (pp. 29–34). In the novels,
such transformations are effected by placing characters
from different temporal planes into a distinct set of
narrative segments. When Kathie becomes a youth, a
stage direction states that she and Juan "suffer a transformation: they appear as two youths, chatting on a
neighborhood street corner."[19] (This stage direction does
not explain, however, precisely *how* the characters "suffer" the transformation onstage.) As for Santiago, his
principal role is that of humble professor transformed
into the suave and dynamic Mark Griffin. The end of
Act I underlines the two main characters' essence as
players of roles in constant transformations. Kathie
states, "Oh, how rapidly the two hours passed today,"
and Santiago responds, "Yes, flying. But we work well,
no, Kathie?" (p. 82). Near the end of the work, Kathie
calls her apartment a "room of lies" (p. 140), a description that could be used to portray such spaces of multiple transformation as the Green House in the novel of
that title or the bar The Cathedral in the later novel.

    The dialogues in *Kathie y el hipopótamo* some-
times function in a fashion similar to the telescoped
dialogues initially apparent in *The Time of the Hero*
and then fully employed in the later novels. When Santiago and Kathie are speaking, for example, their conversation leads to an interchange between Kathie and

Juan similar to the telescoped dialogues of the novels:

SANTIAGO: Let's erase it, then. From what point don't
you like it?
KATHIE: From the point where the guy approaches me.
JUAN: Guy? You must mean lover.

The dialogue between Santiago and Kathie in the
present changes into an exchange in the past between
Kathie and Juan. The effect of these constant transformations is to make relative and subjective any fixed
interpretation of "objective" reality. The reader or observer's understanding of characters and situations is
regularly placed into doubt by a competing and even
contradictory version of things emanating from many
sources.

Vargas Llosa explains in a preface how this should
appear before the spectator's eyes in *Kathie y el hipopótamo*: "The work's action transgresses the conventional limits of normality and occurs in the objective
and subjective world as if they were one, moving with
complete liberty in one and another direction." This
vision of reality ultimately leads the observer of these
plays to conclude, like the reader of Vargas Llosa's novels, that his fictional and theatrical worlds are con-
sumed with the irrational. As Belisario concludes, simply, near the end of *La señorita de Tacna*: " . . . there
are things that aren't understandable" (p. 137).

Another sphere of confluence of Vargas Llosa's fiction and these plays is his integration of popular forms
of fiction: the melodrama of the soap opera and the
adventure of the traditional novel of chivalry. Both dramatic works contain elements that catalyze these popular forms. In *La señorita de Tacna* Belisario strives to
write a simple "love story." His very first line in the play,
in fact, emphasizes this intention: "What are you doing
in a love story, Mamaé?" (p. 22). Throughout the play

he continues to speak regularly of his "love story" or "romantic story." The simple story he desires, however, seems to consistently evade him, and finally results in a series of rather scandalous revelations about the family. Phrased in the terms of popular fiction, his idealized love story of the movies has turned into the vulgar material of the most banal television soap operas. There are several stories that are qualitatively different in *Kathie y el hipopótamo*. The anecdotes that appear at the beginning of each act and at the end of the play, nevertheless, are of an adventure worthy of the *Amadis de Gaula* or *Tirant lo Blanc*: Kathie and Santiago relate an intriguing story located in an exotic Egypt and other distant lands. In both of his theatrical pieces Vargas Llosa juxtaposes a supposedly "pure" story (a "pure" love story and the quintessential adventure story) with the harsh realities of everyday life in contemporary Peruvian society.

Vargas Llosa has discussed the "total novel" in his essays, as noted, and has written works such as *Conversation in The Cathedral* and *The War of the End of the World* that seemingly aspire to such grandiose comprehensiveness. He explains in his introductory remarks to *Kathie y el hipopótamo* that his totalization impulse was a factor for him in this play: "Perhaps it isn't necessary to say that in this farce I have attempted, as in my novels, to attain an illusion of totality. 'Total' should be understood in a qualitative and not quantitative manner in this case." Vargas Llosa further develops this concept by explaining that the play does not attempt to represent human experience extensively, but rather to show that it is at once objective and subjective, real and unreal.

This distinction between the quantitative and the qualitative is important for the comparison of his fiction and theater. *Kathie y el hipopótamo* shares with

the early novels an exploration of both objective and
subjective planes of reality. Considering this concept in
a quantitative fashion, the reader would find it difficult to compare the play with *Conversation in The
Cathedral* or *The War of the End of the World*. The
play, rather, seems like a mere sketch for one of Vargas
Llosa's ambitiously "total novels." Just as a superficial
filmscript served as the catalyst for the extensive novel,
the two plays can be seen as sketches for two potentially
exhaustive works of fiction. These "total novels" would
more appropriately accommodate Vargas Llosa's own
description of the "total" work as delineated in his essays than would the two plays.

Within the context of Vargas Llosa's fiction a discussion of these two plays brings into question certain
issues of a more theatrical nature, which have been discussed briefly in the analyses of his novels: the issues of
oral versus written culture, and the function of storytelling. The fact that theater is presented orally and
novels appear in written form brings to mind this issue.
Walter Ong would maintain that modern theater is a
product of written culture: a playwright *writes* a script
from which the actors memorize their (written) lines.[20]
In addition, many plays, such as the two in question
here, are published as written texts that are not only
read, but are intended to be read just as is a novel.

The dynamics of oral versus written culture is
operational in both plays. *La señorita de Tacna* opens
with a visual image of these two cultures in action. The
spectator first perceives a dark stage and Mamaé's *voice*
(oral); then her face is illuminated. The sound of her
voice and the visual image of her face emphasize her
role as the oral communicator in the play. After she
makes a brief six-line statement, the stage is totally
illuminated and the spectator sees Belisario as the image of written culture — "seated at his work table, writ-

ing furiously." Belisario's task, as the play progresses, is to accommodate Mamaé's oral stories to the one written story he is attempting to fabricate. In *Kathie y el hipopótamo* the play opens with Kathie and Santiago orally relating their adventure story into a tape recorder. In respect for the oral form of storytelling, they prefer to relate the event verbally (with the assumed intention of later transcribing it into written form). Santiago's existence and the development of the play around him is a function of the oral versus the written. His role as Mark Griffin is a product of his and Kathie's oral story; his idealized character in this invented story is the perfect product of written culture: as Kathie points out, Santiago and his friends "have read all books and know everything" (p. 77).

The synthesis of oral and written culture is found in the form of story. This synthesis is the ultimate accommodation of these two disparate elements in the two plays. It is evident from the prefatory remarks in *Kathie y el hipopótamo* that Vargas Llosa is increasingly interested in the function of story in society and in the human psyche: "When I wrote this work I didn't know that its profound theme was the relationship between life and fiction, an alchemy which fascinates me because the more I practice fiction the less I understand it." In commentary preceding *La señorita de Tacna* he had already proposed a vital function for story: "The story is one of few forms — perhaps the only one — capable of expressing that unity of the man who lives and dreams, of reality and desires."

The most significant event in *La señorita de Tacna* is Belisario's discovery of how to write a story. He spends much of the play struggling to write a "love story," imagining his final product in terms of previously conceived formulas. Consequently, he struggles throughout the play to adapt the characters' actions to the different types of stories he believes these actions require. Constantly establishing his own fixed parameters for the proposed story, Belisario finds creation impossible: at the end of Act I he exclaims in frustration that he is "incapable of finishing a story," and falls asleep at the end of the first act — an absolute failure as storyteller. At the beginning of Act II Belisario continues his mistaken approach to the creation of fiction, continuing to work on fixed models and complaining that Mamaé is not providing him with sufficient *details*: "You always leave me starving for details." As Act II progresses, Belisario arrives at some fundamental revelations about the act of creation. In one of his soliloquies he states: " . . . a writer is he who writes, not what he wants to write — that is the normal man — but rather what his demons want". He has realized that the material at hand will dictate the story to him, and not vice versa. The play ends with Belisario's conclusions:

It isn't a love story, it isn't a romantic story. What is it then? . . . Since I didn't know the true story, I have had to add things that I remembered, and others that I invented and robbed from here and there . . .

Mamaé's details are no longer necessary, as Belisario has learned. He has concluded that writing is, in effect, an act controlled by the creative imagination and the "demons" that Vargas Llosa has discussed in his essays. By integrating oral anecdotes and elements of his own psyche into written form, Belisario synthesizes oral and written culture into story. These oral and written dynamics, and their relationship to story, are the true essence of this play and a key element in Vargas Llosa's own creative process in his fiction. It is within this framework that his theater is most enlightening in the context of his total work.

The Real Life of Alejandro Mayta (1984)

Like Belisario in *La señorita de Tacna* — who had a
story imposed upon him — Vargas Llosa seems to have
responded quite directly to what he would probably
call historical or political "demons" when he penned
The Real Life of Alejandro Mayta. The recent political
situation in Peru, dominated by unmitigated violence,
is dealt with directly in this novel. Vargas Llosa has
explained the background as follows: "I have tried to
express something . . . Something that will avoid this
accommodation to horror of my compatriots. Tombs of
assassinated groups, terrifying executions of women
and children, entire towns wiped out . . . "[21] The new
novel can be seen as a result of a political violence
beginning in 1962 and culminating in a much-publi-
cized massacre of eight journalists in 1983.

The massacre was fully exposed to international
scrutiny when Vargas Llosa himself published an article in Peru's *Oiga*, which ran later, in translation, in the
New York Times Magazine.[22] He had been commis-
sioned by the Peruvian government to investigate the
gruesome series of events that took place in Uchuraccay, an Indian village near Ayacucho southeast of Lima
in the Andes. His article explains how eight reporters
from a variety of newspapers decided to investigate a
story concerning guerrillas of the Sendero Luminoso
("Shining Path") and reportedly were killed by villagers
in Huaychao. The area was tense with conflict between
guerrillas and the military, and had been a strong in-
road for the Sendero Luminoso; it is not difficult to
imagine how the identity of the journalists became a
confused issue, resulting in their deaths, primarily out
of ignorance and misunderstanding. Vargas Llosa has
been deeply affected by Peru's recent history of violence: "This is what I wanted, at least in my novel, to

be clear: that violence at a certain point lacks ideology."[23]

The key event in *The Real Life of Alejandro Mayta* takes place not in Uchuraccay but in Jauja, and it has a historical base. In 1958 an armed rebellion in this Andean village failed in its goal to overthrow the government. In fact, it was a disorganized and ill-conceived local uprising in which the majority of the participants were high-school students; an aged Trotskyite and an impulsive young idealist had orchestrated the event. Soon after the publication of the novel, a Peruvian magazine published an article about the person on whom Vargas Llosa's character Mayta is principally based: Jacinto Rentería.[24] According to this article, Rentería was the Trotskyite in the Jauja uprising.

Vargas Llosa's *The Real Life of Alejandro Mayta* is a ten-chapter novel that features Mayta and a novelist as its main characters. The novelist, who appears to be Mario Vargas Llosa himself, but is never named, is the narrator within the story. The narrator-novelist relates, in the present tense, conditions in Peru and his efforts to reconstruct Mayta's story. He attempts to carry out this task by soliciting and listening to the testimonies of persons who had known Mayta under various circumstances. Each chapter features, primarily, one person's version of Mayta's life; the last chapter is an encounter between the novelist and Mayta.

Those whom the novelist seeks out include his ex-girlfriend, Jauja's eminent Marxist professor, a leftist Peruvian senator, and several political collaborators. As could be expected, many of their anecdotes and ideas about Mayta are contradictory. Some portray him as revolutionary and ideological; others, as an emotional young man unable to define a political position and who even worked with the CIA. While most believe he was the organizer of the Jauja disaster, some describe his participation in Jauja as marginal. His ex-girlfriend

affirms that Mayta is homosexual; Mayta disclaims this
to the narrator-novelist. Even though it is to be expected that different persons would present varying points
of view on Mayta, at the conclusion of the novel he is
seen simply as a contradictory and confused individual
who failed in gaining whatever political objectives he
might have had.

The contemporary Peru of the narrator-novelist's
"present" is a poor and strife-ridden nation seemingly
headed toward absolute chaos. The narrator-novelist
occasionally contemplates the situation, and cannot
avoid noticing his surroundings as he moves from witness to witness. In one scene he briefly observes the
working poor whose modest and monotonous lives are
good fortune in comparison to the unemployed and
destitute street people of Lima.[25] According to the senator, the social and political deterioration in Peru has
reached new extremes (p. 110). The general malaise
and violent rural situation portray a nation on the
verge of collapse.

When Vargas Llosa was a child living in Bolivia,
he imagined a fictional Peru populated by heroic Incas.
Four decades later, he has invented a vastly different
country, but has still presented a basically fictional and
literary nation. It is literary not because its people are
culturally sophisticated but because its reality is communicated and understood in a literary fashion: "Since
it is impossible to know what's really happening, we
Peruvians lie, invent, dream, and take refuge in illusion. Because of these strange circumstances, Peruvian
life in which so few people actually do read, has become literary" (p. 246). There are several other allu-
sions to Peru as this fictional entity. The narrator also
remarks frequently that his goal is not to write "true
history," but to use the multiple and contradictory versions of Mayta's life to fabricate a story. He notes:
"One thing you learn, when you try to reconstruct an

event from eyewitness accounts, is that each version is just someone's story, and that all stories mix truth and lies." (p. 118)

Vargas Llosa has explained his ambiguous relationship with Peru on several occasions, describing how the nation is a "passion" and "disease" for him; it is a phenomenon that has the emotion and nuances of a love–hate relationship. After a hiatus of over a decade — marked by excursions into humor and into nineteenth-century Brazil — Vargas Llosa returns to his passion by making Peru itself the central topic of *The Real Life of Alejandro Mayta*. Consequently, this could logically be one of the works to which he feels most closely attached. It is a well-written novel that tells a significant story in the context of the "demons" that Vargas Llosa claims he has spent his career exorcising. Nevertheless, *The Real Life of Alejandro Mayta* is a minor work in the scheme of Vargas Llosa's fiction: it has neither the breadth nor the profundity of his previous novels.

Conclusion

Vargas Llosa is a modern rather than post-modern writer. In contrast to the purely self-reflective and frequently empty narcissism of the post-modernist, he is a novelist of substance. He is a storyteller in the Faulknerian tradition that so pervasively affected Latin America during the 1940s and 1950s. This type of fiction, identified by one critic as transcendent regionalism in Spanish-American literature, has been practiced in a variety of ways by writers such as Gabriel García Márquez and Juan Rulfo, as well as by Vargas Llosa and a host of others.[1] Vargas Llosa has never questioned the act of storytelling itself, but rather has sought to clarify in his essays and theater how the writer creates, and what function story and storytelling have in society.

His stature as a major writer of the twentieth century is testified to by his broad international appeal. The reader finds in Vargas Llosa's writing all three of the basic values that Wayne C. Booth has proposed as the possible interests of fiction: intellectual, qualitative, and practical.[2] The intellectual interest in his novels concerns numerous facets of Peruvian and Latin American society. The qualitative is seen, as the varying patterns of the novels unfold, in the incorporation of varying literary traditions, such as realism, romance, and the fictional style of Faulkner, among others. The constant practical interest in Vargas Llosa's novels lies in plot development, suspense, and the resolution of character development.

Several characteristics of Vargas Llosa's themes and techniques contribute to his universality. The interest in the "total novel" noted in Chapter 4's analysis of *Conversation in The Cathedral*, but present in varying degrees in much of his work, makes him comparable to a group of classic writers that would include such names as Balzac, Tolstoy, and, once again, Faulkner. The successful development and incorporation of romance — from the early stories through *The Green House* and *The War of the End of the World* — distinguishes him from many Latin American writers who share his political and social perspectives but produce a more overtly "social" literature. His use of heteroglossia to create many-languaged texts should be viewed as the adept manipulation of the many languages that the contemporary Latin American novelist has at his disposal, writing in a society without linguistic, literary, or social unity. Most of Vargas Llosa's techniques, especially his use of dialogue, narrative point of view, and time, can be considered a particular and sometimes refined application of innovations originally heralded by Joyce, Dos Passos, and Faulkner. The use of focalisers, analyzed in *Conversation in The Cathedral* and *The War of the End of the World*, however, represents an exceptionally intricate and effective manipulation of technique even for a modern writer. The structures and methods of narrative found in all his novels share in making the reader of Vargas Llosa an active participant in a continually direct, seemingly unmediated experience.

Vargas Llosa belongs to a disappearing species in the United States, still extant in Latin America: the "man of letters." His novels, essays, and theater confirm this status as a writer whose interests — in a society that increasingly fosters overspecialization — are wide ranging. Always concerned and deeply involved with local and national issues, Vargas Llosa has nonetheless maintained an international vision with respect to the literature and politics which remain indispensable disciplines for many Latin American writers. He is also a man of passions. Nevertheless, whatever Vargas Llosa's creative, scholarly, or personal passions may have been throughout his career, they are secondary to the paramount and unparalleled passion of his life and career: storytelling.

Notes

1. The History of a Passion:
Introduction to Mario Vargas Llosa

1. José Miguel Oviedo has documented Vargas Llosa's feelings about the discipline of writing and his admiration of Flaubert in *Mario Vargas Llosa: la invención de una realidad* (Barcelona: Seix Barral, 1970). See especially pages 62–69.
2. John S. Brushwood, *The Spanish American Novel: A Twentieth Century Survey* (Austin and London: University of Texas Press, 1975), p. 254.
3. See Oviedo, pp. 223–30.
4. See Brushwood, p. 329.
5. Brushwood discusses the new direction set forth with the publication of these four Spanish-American novels in *The Spanish American Novel*, pp. 157–79.
6. Mario Vargas Llosa, "*Sebastián Salazar Bondy y la vocación del escritor en el Perú*," in *Contra viento y marea* (Barcelona: Seix Barral/Biblioteca Breve, 1984), p. 92.
7. John S. Brushwood discusses *Aves sin nido* as a landmark novel in *Genteel Barbarism: New Readings of Nineteenth-Century Spanish-American Novels* (London and Lincoln: University of Nebraska Press, 1981), p. 139.
8. Vargas Llosa has published a book on Arguedas, *José María Arguedas, entre sapos y halcones* (Madrid: Edi-

ciones Cultura Hispánica del Centro Iberoamericano de Cooperación, 1978).

9. Vargas Llosa, "*Sebastián Salazar Bondy y la vocación del escritor en el Perú*."

10. John S. Brushwood provides an overview of twentieth-century Peruvian history in *The Spanish-American Novel*, pp. 190 and 327–28.

11. D. P. Gallagher, *Modern Latin American Literature* (London, Oxford, and New York: Oxford University Press, 1973), p. 122.

12. Vargas Llosa made this statement in *Marcha* (Montevideo), No. 1553 (July 23, 1971), p. 31. D. P. Gallagher quotes and translates this statement into English in *Modern Latin American Literature*, pp. 122.

13. Mario Vargas Llosa, "A Passion for Peru," *New York Times Magazine* (November 20, 1983), p. 106.

14. Brushwood, *The Spanish American Novel*, pp. 327–28.

15. Vargas Llosa, "A Passion for Peru," p. 79.

16. *Ibid.*, p. 97.

17. *Ibid.*, p. 99.

18. *Ibid.*, p. 99.

19. Oviedo, *Mario Vargas Llosa: invención de una realidad*, p. 21.

20. *Ibid.*, p. 25.

21. Mario Vargas Llosa, "*En Cuba, País Sitiado*," and "*Crónica de una revolución*," in *Contra viento y marea*, pp. 21–29 and 30–35.

22. Oviedo, *Mario Vargas Llosa: la invención de una realidad*, p. 29.

23. Vargas Llosa, "A Passion for Peru," p. 108.

24. Mario Vargas Llosa, "*La censura en la URSS y Alexander Solzhenitsen*," and "*Un caso de censura en Gran Bretaña*," in *Contra viento y marea*, pp. 126–30 and 140–44.

25. Mario Vargas Llosa, "*Luzbel y otras conspiraciones*," in *Contra viento y marea*, pp. 150–59.

26. Mario Vargas Llosa, "*El socialismo y los tanques*," in *Contra viento y marea*, pp. 160–63.

27. Vargas Llosa, "A Passion for Peru," p. 110.

2. The Beginnings: The Early Stories (1959)
and *The Time of the Hero* (1963)

1. Author's Preface, *The Cubs and Other Stories* (New York, Hagerstown, San Francisco, and London: Harper and Row, 1979), p. xiii.
2. *Ibid.*, p. xv.
3. The volume in English *The Cubs and Other Stories* is not identical to the book in which these early stories first appeared in Spanish as *Los jefes*. *Los jefes* was published in 1959 with the following stories: "*Los jefes*" (The Leaders), "*El desafío*"(The Challenge), "*El hermano menor*" (The Younger Brother), "*Día domingo*" (On Sunday), "*Un visitante*" (A Visitor), and "*El abuelo*" (The Grandfather).
4. Mario Vargas Llosa, *The Cubs and Other Stories* (New York, Hagerstown, San Francisco, and London: Harper and Row, 1979), p. 49. All quotations in English of the stories discussed in this chapter are from this edition and henceforth are noted parenthetically in the text.
5. *Ibid.*, p. xv.
6. See Susan S. Lanser, *The Narrative Act: Point of View in Prose Fiction* (Princeton: Princeton University Press, 1981), p. 101.
7. Mikhail Bakhtin defines heteroglossia as a many-languaged discourse in *the Dialogic Imagination* (Austin and London: University of Texas Press, 1981), p. 428.
8. See Jorge Lafforgue, "*La ciudad y los perros, novela moral,*" in *Nueva novela latinoamericana I* (Buenos Aires: Editorial Paidós, 1976). This article was published originally in 1965.
9. *Ibid.*, p. 238.
10. Oviedo, *Mario Vargas Llosa: la invención de una realidad*, p. 99.
11. Sharon Magnarelli has analyzed the "I" narrator of *The Time of the Hero* in "*The Time of the Hero*: Liberty Enslaved," *Latin American Literary Review*, Vol. 4, No. 8 (Spring–Summer 1976) pp. 35–45.
12. See Meir Sternberg, *Expositional Modes and Temporal*

Ordering in Fiction (Baltimore: Johns Hopkins University Press, 1978).

13. Mario Vargas Llosa, *The Time of the Hero*, translated by Lysander Kemp (New York: Grove Press, 1966), p. 201. All quotations are from this edition and henceforth are noted parenthetically in the text.

14. In the original Spanish the distinction is clearer since the punctuation sets the first sentence apart.

15. See Magnarelli, "*The Time of the Hero*: Liberty Enslaved," pp. 37–38.

16. Roy Kerr has discussed Boa in more detail in "The Secret Self: Boa in Vargas Llosa's *La ciudad y los perros*," *Romance Notes*, Vol. 24, No. 2 (1984), pp. 1–5.

3. Maturity: *The Green House* (1965) and *The Cubs* (1967)

1. Oviedo, *Mario Vargas Llosa: la invención de una realidad*, p. 122; George McMurray, "The Novels of Mario Vargas Llosa," *Modern Language Quarterly*, Vol. 29, No. 3 (1968): 329–40.

2. Mario Vargas Llosa, *Historia secreta de una novela* (Barcelona: Tusquets, 1971), p. 8.

3. See Alexander Coleman, "The Transfiguration of the Chivalric Novel," *World Literature Today*, Vol. 52, No. 2 (Winter 1978), p. 24.

4. Vargas Llosa, *Historia secreta de una novela*, p. 24.

5. Mario Vargas Llosa, *The Green House*, translated by Gregory Rabassa (New York: Avon Books, 1973), p. 247. All quotations are from this edition and henceforth are noted parenthetically in the text.

6. Luys A. Díez has interviewed Vargas Llosa concerning the background to *The Green House* and visited Piura and the Amazon jungle. He spoke, for example, with the Indian chieften Jum. See Díez, "The Sources of *The Green House*: The Mythical Background of a Fabulous Novel," in Charles Rossman and Alan Warren Friedman, *Mario Vargas Llosa* (Austin and London: University of Texas Press, 1978), pp. 36–51.

7. *Ibid.*, p. 43.

8. Elena Poniatowska, *"Al fin un escritor que le pasiona escribir, no lo que se diga de sus libros: Mario Vargas Llosa,"* La cultura en Mexico (supplement to *Siempre*), No. 117 (July 7, 1965), p. 3.

9. See Michael Moody, "A Small Whirlpool: Narrative Structure in *The Green House,"* Texas Studies in Literature and Language, Vol. 19, No. 4 (Winter 1977), p. 415.

10. *Ibid.*, p. 416.

11. *Ibid.*, pp. 424–25.

12. Some readers may not read these passages strictly as interior monologues. Moody does not view them as interior monologues, but admits that they could be read as such. Vargas Llosa himself has proposed in his *Historia secreta de una novela* that they represent a generalized speech of the townfolk. In the most precise terms, these ambiguous passages should be described as alternating between Anselmo's interior monologues and the speech of unidentified persons in the town.

13. Michael Moody has used these categories of Lord Raglan to define Don Anselmo as a hero. See Moody, "Don Anselmo and the Myth of the Hero in *La casa verde,"* The International Fiction Review, No. 4 (1977), pp. 186–89.

14. Wolfgang A. Luchting has proposed the term "mythologizing" (*mitizante*) in *"Los mitos y lo mitizante en La casa verde,"* Mundo Nuevo, No. 43 (January 1970), pp. 56–60.

15. Michael Moody, "A Small Whirlpool: Narrative Structure in *The Green House,"* p. 412.

16. See Michael Moody, "Web of Defeat: A Thematic View of Characterization in Mario Vargas Llosa's *La casa verde,"* Hispania, Vol. 59, No. 1 (March 1970), p. 19.

17. Roy Kerr has discussed the use of choral characters in "Choral Characters in Mario Vargas Llosa's Early Novels," *Prisma/Cabral*, Fall 1983, pp. 66–75.

18. See Michael Moody, "A Verbal Reality: Stylistic Method in Vargas Llosa's *La casa verde," Symposium*, Vol. 32, No. 4 (Winter 1978), p. 312.

19. *Ibid.*, p. 312.

20. *Ibid.*, p. 312.

21. The Champs' theme song is recounted in Spanish as follows: "*Eran los inconquistables, no sabían trabajar, solo chupar, solo timbear, eran los inconquistables y ahora iban a culear.*" Translated literally, it reads: "They were the Champs, they didn't know how to work, only drink, only play cards, they were the Champs and now they were going to fuck."

22. The invention of words such as "bestest" in English is an attempt at translating the *mangache* special use of superlatives in Spanish.

23. Richard Chase defines romance as such in *The American Novel and Its Traditions* (New York: Doubleday Anchor, 1957), pp. 12–13.

24. René Wellek and Austin Warren, *Theory of Literature*, 2nd rev. ed. (New York: Harcourt, Brace, Jovanovich, 1956), p. 216.

25. See Coleman, "The Transfiguration of the Chivalric Novel."

26. See Michael Moody, "A Small Whirlpool: Narrative Structure in *The Green House,*" pp. 408–28.

27. Mario Vargas Llosa, *The Cubs and Other Stories*, p. xvii.

28. *Ibid.*, pp. xvii–xviii.

29. *Ibid.*, p. xviii.

30. Julio Ortega, *La contemplación y la fiesta* (Caracas: Monte Ávila, 1969), p. 138.

31. Wolfgang A. Luchting has made this observation concerning the passage of time in *Mario Vargas Llosa: desarticulador de realidades* (Bogotá: Plaza y Janes, 1978), p. 114.

32. *Ibid.*, p. 114.

33. Ortega, *La contemplación y la fiesta*, pp. 145–47.

34. Mario Vargas Llosa, *Los cachorros* (Barcelona: Editorial Lumen, 1967), p. 105.

4. Peruvian Epic: *Conversation in The Cathedral* (1967)

1. Ricardo Cano Gaviria, *El buitre y el ave fénix: conversación con Mario Vargas Llosa* (Barcelona: Anagrama, 1972), p. 73.

2. Alan Cheuse, "Mario Vargas Llosa and *Conversation in The Cathedral*: The Question of Naturalism," in Rossman and Friedman, *Mario Vargas Llosa*, pp. 52–58.

3. Michael Wood, "Masquerades," *New York Review of Books* (March 30, 1975), pp. 27–28.

4. Oviedo, *Mario Vargas Llosa: la invención de una realidad*, pp. 183–84.

5. *Ibid.*, p. 184.

6. Mary Davis, "Mario Vargas Llosa: The Necessary Scapegoat," in Rossman and Friedman, *Mario Vargas Llosa*, pp. 145.

7. Robert Brody, "Mario Vargas Llosa and the Totalization Impulse," in Rossman and Friedman, *Mario Vargas Llosa*, pp. 120–27.

8. Luis Harss and Barbara Dohmann, *Into the Mainstream* (New York: Harper and Row, 1966), p. 361.

9. Oviedo, *Mario Vargas Llosa: la invención de una realidad*, p. 96.

10. Wolfgang A. Luchting, "*Los fracasos de Mario Vargas Llosa*," *Mundo Nuevo*, Nos. 51–52 (September–October 1970), 61–72.

11. Randolph Pope provides an overview of the criticism on this question in "*Precauciones para la lectura de Conversación en La Catedral*," *Journal of Spanish Studies: Twentieth Century*, Vol. 6, No. 3 (Winter 1978), pp. 207–17.

12. Ricardo Cano Gaviria, *El buitre y el ave fénix*, pp. 96–98.

13. José Luis Martín, *La narrativa de Vargas Llosa: un acercamiento estilístico* (Madrid: Gredos, 1974), p. 249.

14. Alan Cheuse, "Mario Vargas Llosa and *Conversation in The Cathedral*," in Rossman and Friedman, *Mario Vargas Llosa*, p. 52.

15. *Ibid.*, p. 58.

16. Jean Franco, "Conversations and Confessions: Self and Character in *The Fall* and *Conversation in The Cathedral*," in Rossman and Friedman, *Mario Vargas Llosa*, pp. 59–75.

17. *Ibid.*, p. 60.

18. *Ibid.*, p. 64.

19. *Ibid.*, p. 74.

20. Mary Davis, "Mario Vargas Llosa: The Necessary Scapegoat," in Rossman and Friedman, *Mario Vargas Llosa*, pp. 136–50.

21. *Ibid.*, p. 43.

22. Mario Vargas Llosa, *Conversation in The Cathedral* translated by Gregory Rabassa (New York, Evanston, San Francisco, and London: Harper and Row, 1975), p. 137. All quotations in English are from this edition and henceforth are noted parenthetically in the text.

23. Mario Vargas Llosa, *Conversación en La Catedral* (Barcelona: Seix Barral, 1969), p. 73. All quotations in Spanish are from this edition and henceforth are noted parenthetically in the text.

24. Michael Wood, "Masquerades," p. 27.

25. Oviedo, *Mario Vargas Llosa: la invención de una realidad*, p. 226.

26. *Ibid.*, p. 227.

27. Gérard Genette, "*Discours du récit*," in *Figures III* (Paris: Seuil, 1972). In the introduction, Genette sets forth the possibility of considering a story on the basis of the expansion of a verb. For example, Genette notes that in *The Odyssey* the verb would be "Ulysses returns to Ithaca," and, in Proust's *À la Recherche du temps perdu*, "Marcel becomes a writer."

28. Ronald Christ, "*La novela y cine: Vargas Llosa, entre Flaubert y Eisenstein*," *El Urogallo*, Nos. 35–36 (September 1975), pp. 115–20.

29. Michael Wood, "Masquerades," p. 27.

30. Oviedo, *Mario Vargas Llosa: la invención de una realidad*, p. 226.

31. Fredric Jameson, *The Political Unconscious: Narrative as a Socially Symbolic Act* (Ithaca and London: Cornell University Press, 1981). See especially p. 144.

32. Susan S. Lanser, *The Narrative Act*, p. 101.

33. See Charles David Bevelander, "Point of View in Mario Vargas Llosa's *Conversación en La Catedral*," doctoral dissertation, University of Illinois, 1975, p. 220.

34. I have used the term "omniscient narrator outside the story" in accordance with recent clarifications in narratology carried out by Gérard Genette. Genette has de-

monstrated how the terms "first-person" and "third-person" narrators are inaccurate. He points out that, technically speaking, all narrators are "first-person"; the real question is whether the narrator is inside or outside the story. See Gérard Genette, *Figures III* (Paris: Seuil, 1972), p. 203.

35. Bevelander, p. 219.
36. Mieke Bal, "*Narration et focalisation: pour une théorie des instances du récit*," *Poétique*, Vol. 29 (1972), pp. 107–27.
37. Charles David Bevelander quotes Walter Rideout in "Point of View in Mario Vargas Llosa's *Conversación en La Catedral*." See Walter Rideout, *The Radical Novel in the United States 1900–1954* (Cambridge, Mass.: Harvard University Press, 1956).
38. José Miguel Oviedo, *Mario Vargas Llosa: la invención de una realidad*, p. 188.
39. *Ibid.*, p. 189.
40. *Ibid.*, p. 199.
41. Jean Franco, "Conversations and Confessions: Self and Character in *The Fall* and *Conversation in The Cathedral*," p. 59.
42. When speaking of a "political novel," I refer to a work that has politics as the subject.

5. The Discovery of Humor: *Captain Pantoja and the Special Service* (1973) and *Aunt Julia and the Script Writer* (1977)

1. Mario Vargas Llosa, *Conversation in The Cathedral*, p. 73.
2. This accessibility of the Spanish-American novel of the 1970s has been discussed in John S. Brushwood, *La novela hispanoamericana del siglo XX: una vista panorámica* (Mexico: Fondo de Cultura Económica, 1984). See especially Chapters 19 through 21, dealing with the 1970s (contributed by Raymond L. Williams).
3. See Gérard Genette, *Figures III*.
4. Mario Vargas Llosa, *Captain Pantoja and the Special*

Service, translated by Ronald Christ and Gregory Kolovakos (New York, Hagerstown, San Francisco, and London: Harper and Row, 1978), pp. 144–45. All quotations in English are from this edition and henceforth are noted parenthetically in the text.

5. José Miguel Oviedo, "A Conversation with Mario Vargas Llosa About *La tía Julia y el escribidor*," in Rossman and Friedman, *Mario Vargas Llosa*, p. 155.

6. *Ibid.*, p. 155.

7. Julia Urquidi Illanes, *Lo que Varguitas no dijo* (What Vargas didn't say) (La Paz: Editorial Khana Cruz, 1985).

8. José Miguel Oviedo, "A Conversation with Mario Vargas Llosa about *La tía Julia y el escribidor*," pp. 157–59.

9. *Ibid* ., p. 159.

10. Mario Vargas Llosa, *Aunt Julia and the Script Writer*, translated by Helen R. Lane (New York: Avon, 1983), p. 17. All quotations are from this edition and henceforth are noted parenthetically in the text.

11. I have published a more detailed analysis of the relationships among the four writers in "*La tía Julia y el escribidor: escritores y lectores*," *Texto crítico*, Vol. 5, No. 13 (April–June 1979), pp. 179–209.

12. Oviedo has applied Roland Barthes's term "scribbler" in "*La tía Julia y el escribidor*: A Self-Coded Portrait," in Rossman and Friedman, *Mario Vargas Llosa*, p. 172.

13. Oviedo, "A Conversation with Mario Vargas Llosa About *La tía Julia y el escribidor*," p. 158.

14. Franz Stanzel, *Narrative Situations in the Novel* (Bloomington: Indiana University Press, 1971).

15. Vargas Llosa discusses these "demons" in *Gabriel García Márquez: historia de un deicidio* (Barcelona and Caracas: Seix Barral and Monte Ávila, 1971), pp. 85–88.

16. Oviedo, "*La tía Julia y el escribidor*: A Coded Self-Portrait," in Rossman and Friedman, *Mario Vargas Llosa*, pp. 167–68.

17. Mario Vargas Llosa, *La orgía perpetua: Flaubert y "Madame Bovary"* (Barcelona: Seix Barral, 1975), p. 18.

18. See José Miguel Oviedo's discussion of Camacho's con-
    fusion of characters in "*La tía Julia y escribidor*: A
    Coded Self-Portrait," in Rossman and Friedman, *Mario
    Vargas Llosa*, pp. 176–77.
19. I have discussed Camacho's use of this formula in more
    detail in my "*La tía Julia y el escribidor: escritores y
    lectores*," pp. 284–97.
20. Mario Vargas Llosa, *La orgía perpetua*, p. 11.
21. See Walter Ong's explanation of how an author fiction-
    alizes readers in "The Writer's Audience is Always a
    Fiction," *PMLA*, Vol. 90, No. 1 (January 1975), pp.
    9–21.
22. Walter Ong analyzes Hemingway's techniques for fic-
    tionalizing a reader in *ibid.*, pp. 12–15.
23. Vargas Llosa, "*Sebastián Salazar Bondy y la vocación
    del escritor en el Perú.*"
24. Jonathan Tittler has discussed *Aunt Julia and the Script
    Writer* within the context of the Spanish-American nov-
    el of the 1970s in *Narrative Irony in the Contemporary
    Spanish-American Novel* (Ithaca and London: Cornell
    University Press, 1984), pp. 129–50.

6. Synthesis: *The War of the End of the World* (1981)

1. Interview with Mario Vargas Llosa, *Washington Post*
   (October 1, 1984), p. B2.
2. *Ibid.*, p. B11.
3. *Ibid.*
4. Ángel Rama, "*La guerra del fin del mundo: una obra
   maestra del fanatismo artístico*," *Eco*, No. 246 (April
   1982), pp. 600–39.
5. Robert Stone, "Revolution as Ritual," *New York Times
   Book Review* (August 12, 1984), pp. 1 and 24.
6. Bruce Allen, *Christian Science Monitor Book Review*
   (October 5, 1984), p. B1.
7. Mario Vargas Llosa, "The Latin-American Novel Today," *Books Abroad*, Vol. 44, No. 1 (Winter 1970), p. 8.
8. Euclides Da Cunha, *Rebellion in the Backlands*, trans-

lated by Samuel Putnam (Chicago and London: University of Chicago Press, 1944), p. 143.

9. *Ibid.*, p. 141.

10. *Ibid.*, p. 177.

11. *Ibid.*, p. 131.

12. *Ibid.*, p. 189.

13. *Ibid.*, p. iii.

14. *Ibid.*, p. 439.

15. Mario Vargas Llosa, *The War of the End of the World*, translated by Helen R. Lane (New York: Farrar, Straus and Giroux, 1984), p. 3. All quotations in English are from this edition and henceforth are noted parenthetically in the text.

16. Alfred MacAdam has compared the two texts in "*Euclides Da Cunha y Mario Vargas Llosa: meditaciones intertextuales,*" *Revista Iberoamericana,*" No. 126 (January–March 1984), pp. 157–64.

17. For a discussion of the military in Vargas Llosa's work, see José Miguel Oviedo, "*Tema del traidor y del héroe: los intelectuales y los militares en Vargas Llosa,*" in José Miguel Oviedo, *Mario Vargas Llosa: el escritor y la crítica* (Madrid: Taurus, 1981), pp. 47–65.

18. Raymond Souza has interpreted the novel's conflicts in "The War of Ideologies in *La guerra del fin del mundo,*" a chapter of a book in preparation.

19. Raymond Souza conceives this battle as a synecdoche in "The War of Ideologies in *La guerra del fin del mundo.*"

20. Mario Vargas Llosa, *La guerra del fin del mundo* (Barcelona: Seix Barral, 1981), p. 227. All quotations in Spanish are from this edition and henceforth are noted parenthetically in the text.

21. M. Bakhtin sets forth the term "dialogic" in *The Dialogic Imagination* (Austin and London: University of Texas Press, 1981).

22. Ángel Rama has studied the function of the narrator in "*La guerra del fin del mundo: una obra maestra del fanatismo artístico,*" p. 608.

23. Mieke Bal formulates the concept of "focaliser" in "*Narration et Focalisation: pour une théorie des instances du recit.*"

24. Oral and written culture as they are being used here have been proposed by Walter Ong in *Orality and Literacy: the Technologizing of the World* (London and New York: Methuen, 1982).

7. Essays, Theater, and
The Real Life of Alejandro Mayta (1984)

1. A recent edition of the English translation of Martorell's *Tirant lo Blanc* includes the following quotation of Vargas Llosa on its back cover: "Martorell is the first of that lineage of God-supplanters—Fielding, Balzac, Dickens, Flaubert, Tolstoy, Joyce, Faulkner—who try to create in their novels an 'all encompassing' reality" (New York: Schocken Books, 1984).
2. Mario Vargas Llosa, *La orgía perpetua*, p. 18.
3. *Ibid.*, pp. 26–27.
4. *Ibid.*, p. 28.
5. *Ibid.*, p. 30.
6. Mario Vargas Llosa, *García Márquez: historia de un deicidio*, p. 85.
7. *Ibid.*, p. 86.
8. *Ibid.*, pp. 479–80.
9. *Ibid.*, p. 480.
10. One telling example of this book's general popularity is the following: during late 1975 and early 1976, the author of these lines was living in Bogotá, Colombia, and both Vargas Llosa's study of Flaubert and, consequently, the Spanish edition of *Madame Bovary* were popular bestsellers.
11. Martín de Riquer and Mario Vargas Llosa, *El combate imaginario: las cartas de batalla de Joanot Martorell* (Barcelona: Barral Editores, 1972).
12. *Ibid.*, p. 26.
13. *Ibid.*, p. 28.
14. Mario Vargas Llosa, *Entre Sartre y Camus* (Rio Piedras, Puerto Rico, 1981), p. 9.
15. *Ibid.*, p. 9.
16. *Ercilla* (Santiago, June 20, 1984), p. 37.
17. *Ibid.*, p. 36.

18. Mario Vargas Llosa, *La señorita de Tacna* (Barcelona: Seix Barral, 1981), p. 9. All quotations are from this edition and henceforth are noted parenthetically in the text.

19. Mario Vargas Llosa, *Kathie y el hipopótamo* (Barcelona: Seix Barral, 1983), p. 19. All quotations are from this edition and henceforth are noted parenthetically in the text.

20. See Walter Ong, *Orality and Literacy: The Technologizing of the World.*

21. Jorge Salazar, "*La nueva novela de Mario Vargas Llosa,*" *Caretas* (November 19, 1984), p. 31.

22. Mario Vargas Llosa, "Inquest in the Andes," *New York Times Magazine* (July 31, 1983), pp. 18–23.

23. Jorge Salzar, "*La nueva novela de Mario Vargas Llosa,*" p. 31.

24. *Ibid.*

25. Mario Vargas Llosa, *The Real Life of Alejandro Mayta* (New York: Farrar, Straus and Giroux, 1986). Translated by Alfred MacAdam, p. 105. All quotations are from this edition and henceforth are noted parenthetically in the text.

Conclusion

1. In *The Spanish-American Novel*, John S. Brushwood has proposed the term "transcendent regionalism" to describe such fiction.

2. Wayne C. Booth, *The Rhetoric of Fiction* (Chicago: University of Chicago Press, 1961), pp. 125–33.

Bibliography

Works by Mario Vargas Llosa

Los jefes. Barcelona: Editorial Rocas, 1959.

La ciudad y los perros. Barcelona: Seix Barral, 1963.

La casa verde. Barcelona: Seix Barral, 1966.

Los cachorros. Barcelona: Editorial Lumen, 1967.

La novela en America Latina: diálogo (with Gabriel García Márquez). Lima: Carlos Milla Batres, 1968.

Conversación en La Catedral. Barcelona: Seix Barral, 1969.

Literatura en la revolución y revolución en la literatura (with Oscar Collazos and Julio Cortázar). México: Siglo XXI, 1970.

Historia secreta de una novela. Barcelona: Tusquets, 1971.

García Márquez: historia de un deicidio. Barcelona: Barral, 1971.

Obras escogidas. Madrid: Aguilar, 1973.

Pantaleón y las visitadoras. Barcelona: Seix Barral, 1973.

El combate imaginario: las cartas de batalla de Joanot Martorell (with Martín de Riquer). Barcelona: Seix Barral, 1973.

García Márquez y la problemática de la novela (with Ángel Rama). Buenos Aires: Corregidor-Marcha, 1973.

La orgía perpetua. Flaubert y "Madame Bovary." Barcelona: Seix Barral, 1975.

La tía Julia y el escribidor. Barcelona: Seix Barral, 1977.

Jose María Arguedas: entre sapos y halcones. Madrid: Ediciones Cultura Hispánica del Centro Iberoamericano de Cooperación, 1978.

La guerra del fin del mundo. Barcelona: Seix Barral, 1981.

Entre Sartre y Camus. Rio Piedras, Puerto Rico: Ediciones Huracan, 1981.
La señorita de Tacna. Barcelona: Seix Barral, 1981.
Contra viento y marea Barcelona: Seix Barral, 1983.
Kathie y el hipopótamo. Barcelona: Seix Barral, 1983.
Historia de Mayta. Barcelona: Seix Barral, 1984.

Translations

The Time of the Hero, trans. Lysander Kemp. New York: Grove Press, 1966.
The Green House, trans. Gregory Rabassa. New York: Avon Books, 1973.
Conversation in The Cathedral, trans. Gregory Rabassa. New York: Harper & Row, 1975.
Captain Pantoja and the Special Service, trans. Ronald Christ and Gregory Kolovakos. New York, Hagerstown, San Francisco, and London: Harper & Row, 1978.
The Cubs and Other Stories, trans. Ronald Christ and Gregory Kolovakos. New York, Hagerstown, San Francisco, and London: Harper & Row, 1979.
Aunt Julia and the Script Writer, trans. Helen R. Lane. New York: Avon Books, 1983.
The War of the End of the World, trans. Helen R. Lane. New York: Farrar, Straus and Giroux, Inc., 1984.
The Real Life of Alejandro Mayta, trans. by Alfred MacAdam. New York: Farrar, Straus and Giroux, Inc., 1986.
Note: I have not included here the hundreds of articles Vargas Llosa has published in newspapers and magazines in Latin America and throughout the world.

Works on Mario Vargas Llosa

Books

Boldori de Baldussi, Rosa. *Vargas Llosa: un narrador y sus demonios*. Buenos Aires: Fernando García Cambeiro, 1974.

Díez, Luis Alfonso. *Mario Vargas Llosa's Pursuit of the Total Novel*. Cuernavaca: CIDOC, Serie Cuadernos No. 2, 1970.

Fernández, Casto M. *Aproximación formal a la novelística de Vargas Llosa*. Madrid: Editora Nacional, 1977.

Gerdes, Dick. *Mario Vargas Llosa*. Boston: G. K. Hall, Twayne World Author Series, 1985.

Giacoman, Helmy F., and Oviedo, José Miguel. *Homenaje a Mario Vargas Llosa*. Madrid: Las Américas, 1972.

Luchting, Wolfgang A. *Mario Vargas Llosa: desarticulador de realidades*. Bogotá: Plaza y Janes, 1978.

Martín, José Luis. *La narrativa de Vargas Llosa: acercamiento estilístico*. Madrid: Gredos, 1974.

Moreno Turner, Fernando. *Para un análisis de la estructura de "La casa verde."* Valparaiso, Chile: Universidad de Chile, 1972.

Oviedo, José Miguel. *Mario Vargas Llosa: la invención de una realidad*. Barcelona: Seix Barral, 1970. 2nd ed. 1977.

_____. *Mario Vargas Llosa: el escritor y la crítica*. Madrid: Taurus Ediciones, 1981.

Rossman, Charles, and Friedman, Alan Warren. *Mario Vargas Llosa: A Collection of Critical Essays*. Austin and London: University of Texas Press, 1978.

Articles

Brody, Robert. "Mario Vargas Llosa and the Totalization Impulse," *Texas Studies in Literature and Language*, Vol. 19, No. 4 (Winter 1977), pp. 514–21.

Cheuse, Alan. "Mario Vargas Llosa and *Conversation in The Cathedral*: The Question of Naturalism," *Texas Studies in Literature and Language*, Vol. 19, No. 4 (Winter 1977), pp. 445–51.

Christ, Ronald. *"La novela y el cine: Vargas Llosa entre Flaubert y Eisenstein,"* *El Urogallo*, Nos. 35–36 (September 1975), 115–20.

Coleman, Alexander. "The Transfiguration of the Chivalric Novel," *World Literature Today*, Vol. 52, No. 1 (1978), pp. 24–30.

Dauster, Frank. "Vargas Llosa and the End of Chivalry,"
    Books Abroad, Vol. 44, No. 1 (1970), pp. 41–45.
Davis, Mary. "Mario Vargas Llosa: The Necessary Scape-
    goat," *Texas Studies in Literature and Language*, Vol.
    19, No. 4 (Winter 1977), pp. 530–44.
Díez, Luys A. "The Sources of *The Green House*: The Mythi-
    cal Background of a Fabulous Novel," *Texas Studies in
    Literature and Language*, Vol. 19, No. 4 (Winter 1977),
    pp. 429–44.
Foster, David William. "*Consideracions estructurales sobre
    La casa verde*," *Norte*, Vol. 12, Nos. 5–6 (October–De-
    cember 1971), pp. 128–35.
Franco, Jean. "Conversations and Confessions: Self and
    Character in *The Fall* and *Conversation in The Cathe-
    dral*," *Texas Studies in Literature and Language*, Vol. 19,
    No. 4 (Winter 1977), pp. 452–68.
Fuentes, Carlos. "*El afán totalizante de Vargas Llosa*," *La
    nueva novela hispanoamericana*. México: Joaquín Mor-
    tiz, 1969, pp. 35–48.
García Pinto, Magdalena. "*Estrategias narrativas y el orden
    temporal en tres novelas de Mario Vargas Llosa*," *Expli-
    cación de Textos Literarios*, Vol. 11, No. 2 (1982–83),
    pp. 41–56.
Kerr, Roy. "Choral Characters in Mario Vargas Llosa's Early
    Novels," *Prisma/Cabral* (Fall 1983), pp. 66–75.
————. "The Secret Self: Boa in Vargas Llosa's *La ciudad y
    los perros*," *Romance Notes*, Vol. 24, No. 2 (1984), pp.
    1–5.
Lafforgue, Jorge. "*Mario Vargas Llosa: moralista*," *Nueva
    novela latinoamericana*, J. Lafforgue ed. Buenos Aires:
    Paidós, 1969, pp. 209–40.
Luchting, Wolfgang A. "*Los mitos y lo mitizante en La casa
    verde*," *Mundo Nuevo*, Vol. 43 (January 1970), pp.
    56–60.
Magnarelli, Sharon. "*The Time of the Hero*: Liberty En-
    slaved," *Latin American Literary Review*, Vol. 4, No. 8
    (Spring–Summer 1976), pp. 35–45.
McMurray, George. "The Novels of Mario Vargas Llosa,"
    Modern Language Quarterly, Vol. 29, No. 3 (1968), pp.
    329–40.

Moody, Michael. "A Small Whirlpool: Narrative Structure in *The Green House*," *Texas Studies in Literature and Language*, Vol. 19, No. 4 (Winter 1977), pp. 408–28.

―――. "Don Anselmo and the Myth of the Hero in *La casa verde*," *The International Fiction Review*, No. 4 (1977), pp. 186–89.

―――. "A Verbal Reality: Stylistic Method in Vargas Llosa's *La casa verde*," *Symposium*, Vol. 32, No. 4 (Winter 1978), pp. 303–27.

Ortega, Julio. "*Los cachorros*," in *La contemplación y la fiesta*, pp. 135–48. Caracas: Monte Ávila, 1969.

Oviedo, José Miguel. "*La tía Julia y el escribidor*: A Coded Self-Portrait," in Charles Rossman and Alan Warren Friedman, *Mario Vargas Llosa*, pp. 166–81. Austin and London: University of Texas Press, 1978.

Pope, Randolph. "*Precauciones para la lectura de Conversación en La Catedral*," *Journal of Spanish Studies: Twentieth Century*, Vol. 6, No. 3 (Winter 1978), pp. 207–17.

Rama, Ángel. "*La guerra del fin del mundo: una obra maestra del fanatismo artístico*," *Eco*, No. 246 (April 1982), pp. 600–39.

Reedy, Daniel. "*Del beso de la mujer araña a la tía Julia: estructura y dinámica interior*," *Revista Iberoamericana*, Vol. 47, Nos. 116–17 (July–December 1980), pp. 109–16.

Rodríguez Monegal, Emir. "*Maudrez de Vargas Llosa*," *Mundo Nuevo*, No. 3 (September 1966), pp. 62–72.

Siemens, William L. "Apollo's Metamorphosis in *Pantaleón y las visitadoras*," *Texas Studies in Literature and Language*, Vol 19, No. 4 (Winter 1977), pp. 481–93.

Williams, Raymond L. "*La tía Julia y el escribidor: escritores y lectores*," *Texto crítico*, Vol. 5, No. 13 (April–June 1979), pp. 179–209.

Index